MEASURING LENGTH

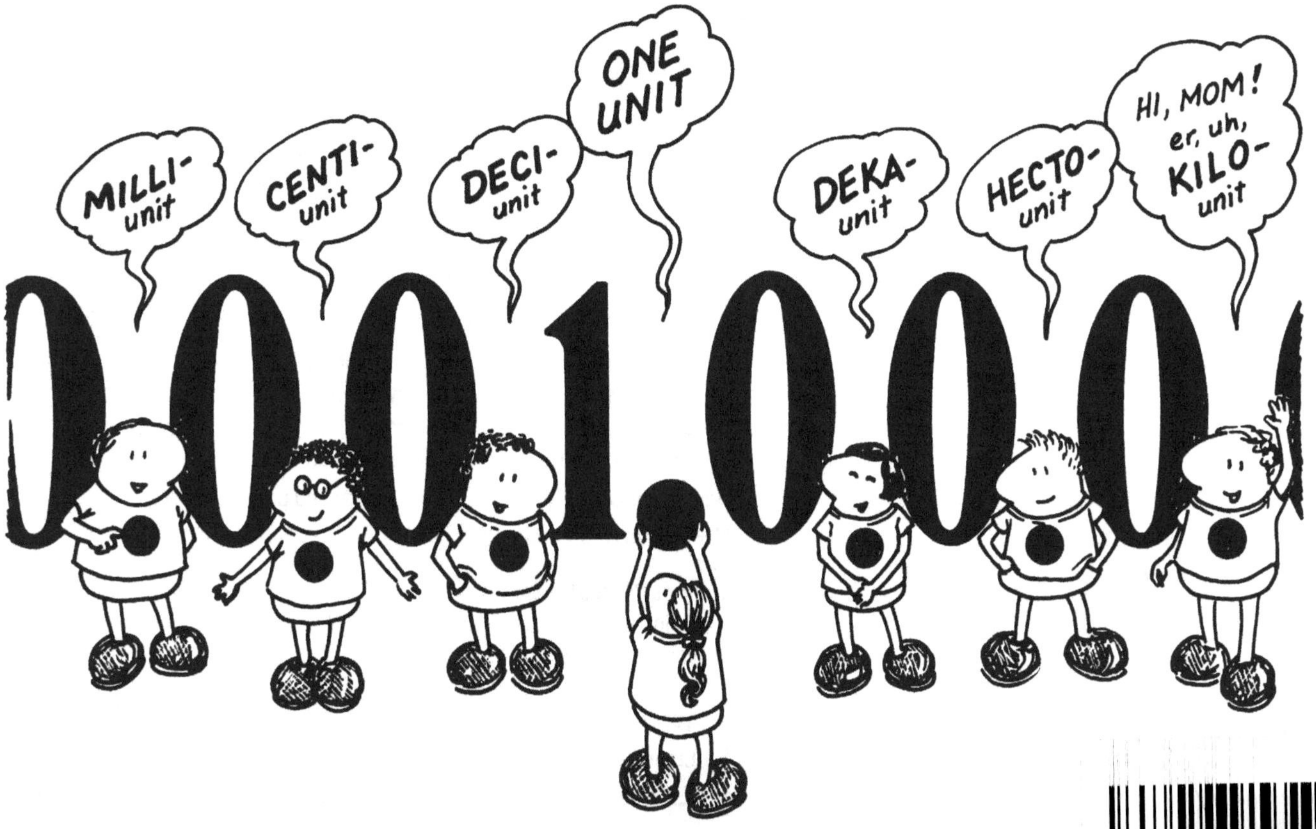

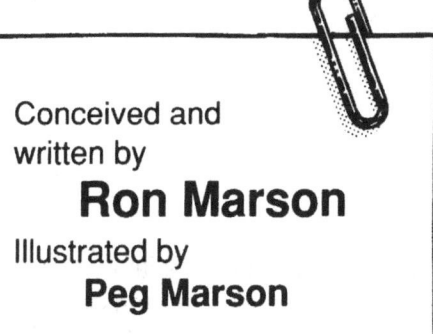

TASK CARD SERIES

Conceived and written by
Ron Marson
Illustrated by
Peg Marson

TOPS LEARNING SYSTEMS

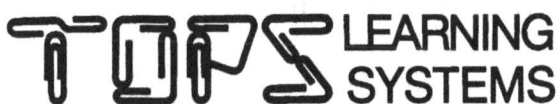

342 S Plumas Street
Willows, CA 95988

www.topscience.org

WHAT CAN YOU COPY?

Dear Educator,

Please honor our copyright restrictions. We offer liberal options and guidelines below with the intention of balancing your needs with ours. When you buy these labs and use them for your own teaching, you sustain our work. If you "loan" or circulate copies to others without compensating TOPS, you squeeze us financially, and make it harder for our small non-profit to survive. Our well-being rests in your hands. Please help us keep our low-cost, creative lessons available to students everywhere. Thank you!

PURCHASE, ROYALTY and LICENSE OPTIONS

TEACHERS, HOMESCHOOLERS, LIBRARIES:

We do all we can to keep our prices low. Like any business, we have ongoing expenses to meet. We trust our users to observe the terms of our copyright restrictions. While we prefer that all users purchase their own TOPS labs, we accept that real-life situations sometimes call for flexibility.

Reselling, trading, or loaning our materials is prohibited unless one or both parties contribute an Honor System Royalty as fair compensation for value received. We suggest the following amounts – let your conscience be your guide.

HONOR SYSTEM ROYALTIES: If making copies from a library, or sharing copies with colleagues, please calculate their value at 50 cents per lesson, or 25 cents for homeschoolers. This contribution may be made at our website or by mail (addresses at the bottom of this page). Any additional tax-deductible contributions to make our ongoing work possible will be accepted gratefully and used well.

Please follow through promptly on your good intentions. Stay legal, and do the right thing.

SCHOOLS, DISTRICTS, and HOMESCHOOL CO-OPS:

PURCHASE Option: Order a book in quantities equal to the number of target classrooms or homes, and receive quantity discounts. If you order 5 books or downloads, for example, then you have unrestricted use of this curriculum for any 5 classrooms or families per year for the life of your institution or co-op.

2-9 copies of any title: 90% of current catalog price + shipping.

10+ copies of any title: 80% of current catalog price + shipping.

ROYALTY/LICENSE Option: Purchase just one book or download *plus* photocopy or printing rights for a designated number of classrooms or families. If you pay for 5 additional Licenses, for example, then you have purchased reproduction rights for an entire book or download edition for any **6** classrooms or families per year for the life of your institution or co-op.

1-9 Licenses: 70% of current catalog price per designated classroom or home.

10+ Licenses: 60% of current catalog price per designated classroom or home.

WORKSHOPS and TEACHER TRAINING PROGRAMS:

We are grateful to all of you who spread the word about TOPS. Please limit copies to only those lessons you will be using, and collect all copyrighted materials afterward. No take-home copies, please. Copies of copies are strictly prohibited.

Copyright © 2000 by TOPS Learning Systems. All rights reserved. This material is created/printed/transmitted in the United States of America. No part of this program may be used, reproduced, or transmitted in any manner whatsoever without written permission from the publisher, *except as explicitly stated above and below*:

The *original owner* of this book or digital download is permitted to make multiple copies of all *student materials* for personal teaching use, provided all reproductions bear copyright notice. A purchasing school or homeschool co-op may assign *one* purchased book or digital download to *one* teacher, classroom, family, or study group *per year*. Reproduction of student materials from libraries is permitted if the user compensates TOPS as outlined above. Reproduction of any copyrighted materials for commercial sale is prohibited.

For licensing, honor system royalty payments, contact: **www.TOPScience.org**; or **TOPS Learning Systems 342 S Plumas St, Willows CA 95988**; or inquire at **customerservice@topscience.org**

ISBN 978-0-941008-72-3

CONTENTS

 **PART I**

INTRODUCTION

A. A TOPS Model for Effective Science Teaching
C. Getting Ready
D. Gathering Materials
E. Sequencing Task Cards
F. Long Range Objectives
G. Review / Test Questions

 **PART II**

TEACHING NOTES

CORE CURRICULUM
1. All Kinds of Measure
2. Metric Prefixes
3. Metric Equivalents
4. Miles and Kilometers
5. Estimate the Last Digit
6. Significant Figures
7. Hairline Measure
8. Agree / Disagree (1)
9. Agree / Disagree (2)
10. Norm Average
11. Long and Short

ENRICHMENT CURRICULUM
12. Rolling Measure
13. Nuts and Bolts (1)
14. Nuts and Bolts (2)
15. To the Moon
16. Line of Sight

 **PART III**

REPRODUCIBLE STUDENT TASK CARDS

Task Cards 1-16
Supplementary Page — Rulers

A TOPS Model for Effective Science Teaching...

If science were only a set of explanations and a collection of facts, you could teach it with blackboard and chalk. You could assign students to read chapters and answer the questions that followed. Good students would take notes, read the text, turn in assignments, then give you all this information back again on a final exam. Science is traditionally taught in this manner. Everybody learns the same body of information at the same time. Class togetherness is preserved.

But science is more than this.

Science is also process — a dynamic interaction of rational inquiry and creative play. Scientists probe, poke, handle, observe, question, think up theories, test ideas, jump to conclusions, make mistakes, revise, synthesize, communicate, disagree and discover. Students can understand science as process only if they are free to think and act like scientists, in a classroom that recognizes and honors individual differences.

Science is *both* a traditional body of knowledge *and* an individualized process of creative inquiry. Science as process cannot ignore tradition. We stand on the shoulders of those who have gone before. If each generation reinvents the wheel, there is no time to discover the stars. Nor can traditional science continue to evolve and redefine itself without process. Science without this cutting edge of discovery is a static, dead thing.

Here is a teaching model that combines the best of both elements into one integrated whole. It is only a model. Like any scientific theory, it must give way over time to new and better ideas. We challenge you to incorporate this TOPS model into your own teaching practice. Change it and make it better so it works for you.

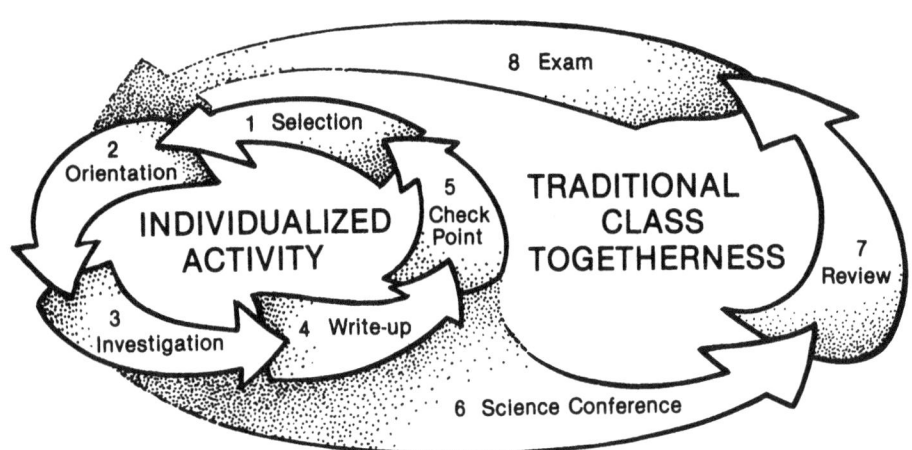

1. SELECTION

Doing TOPS is as easy as selecting the first task card and doing what it says, then the second, then the third, and so on. Working at their own pace, students fall into a natural routine that creates stability and order. They still have questions and problems, to be sure, but students know where they are and where they need to go.

Students generally select task cards in sequence because new concepts build on old ones in a specific order. There are, however, exceptions to this rule: students might *skip* a task that is not challenging; *repeat* a task with doubtful results; *add* a task of their own design to answer original "what would happen if" questions.

2. ORIENTATION

Many students will simply read a task card and immediately understand what to do. Others will require further verbal interpretation. Identify poor readers in your class. When they ask, "What does this mean?" they may be asking in reality, "Will you please read this card aloud?"

With such a diverse range of talent among students, how can you individualize activity and still hope to finish this module as a cohesive group? It's easy. By the time your most advanced students have completed all the task cards, including the enrichment series at the end, your slower students have at least completed the basic core curriculum. This core provides the common background so necessary for meaningful discussion, review and testing on a class basis.

3. INVESTIGATION

Students work through the task cards independently and cooperatively. They follow their own experimental strategies and help each other. You encourage this behavior by helping students only *after* they have tried to help themselves. As a resource person, you work to stay *out* of the center of attention, answering student questions rather than posing teacher questions.

When you need to speak to everyone at once, it is appropriate to interrupt individual task card activity and address the whole class, rather than repeat yourself over and over again. If you plan ahead, you'll find that most interruptions can fit into brief introductory remarks at the beginning of each new period.

4. WRITE-UP

Task cards ask students to explain the "how and why" of things. Write-ups are brief and to the point. Students may accelerate their pace through the task cards by writing these reports out of class.

Students may work alone or in cooperative lab groups. But each one must prepare an original write-up. These must be brought to the teacher for approval as soon as they are completed. Avoid dealing with too many write-ups near the end of the module, by enforcing this simple rule: each write-up must be approved *before* continuing on to the next task card.

5. CHECK POINT

The student and teacher evaluate each write-up together on a pass/no-pass basis. (Thus no time is wasted haggling over grades.) If the student has made reasonable effort consistent with individual ability, the write-up is checked off on a progress chart and included in the student's personal assignment folder or notebook kept on file in class.

Because the student is present when you evaluate, feedback is immediate and effective. A few seconds of this direct student-teacher interaction is surely more effective than 5 minutes worth of margin notes that students may or may not heed. Remember, you don't have to point out every error. Zero in on particulars. If reasonable effort has not been made, direct students to make specific improvements, and see you again for a follow-up check point.

A responsible lab assistant can double the amount of individual attention each student receives. If he or she is mature and respected by your students, have the assistant check the even-numbered write-ups while you check the odd ones. This will balance the work load and insure that all students receive equal treatment.

6. SCIENCE CONFERENCE

After individualized task card activity has ended, this is a time for students to come together, to discuss experimental results, to debate and draw conclusions. Slower students learn about the enrichment activities of faster students. Those who did original investigations, or made unusual discoveries, share this information with their peers, just like scientists at a real conference. This conference is open to films, newspaper articles and community speakers. It is a perfect time to consider the technological and social implications of the topic you are studying.

7. READ AND REVIEW

Does your school have an adopted science textbook? Do parts of your science syllabus still need to be covered? Now is the time to integrate other traditional science resources into your overall program. Your students already share a common background of hands-on lab work. With this shared base of experience, they can now read the text with greater understanding, think and problem-solve more successfully, communicate more effectively.

You might spend just a day on this step or an entire week. Finish with a review of key concepts in preparation for the final exam. Test questions in this module provide an excellent basis for discussion and study.

8. EXAM

Use any combination of the review/test questions, plus questions of your own, to determine how well students have mastered the concepts they've been learning. Those who finish your exam early might begin work on the first activity in the next new TOPS module.

Now that your class has completed a major TOPS learning cycle, it's time to start fresh with a brand new topic. Those who messed up and got behind don't need to stay there. Everyone begins the new topic on an equal footing. This frequent change of pace encourages your students to work hard, to enjoy what they learn, and thereby grow in scientific literacy.

GETTING READY

Here is a checklist of things to think about and preparations to make before your first lesson.

☐ Decide if this TOPS module is the best one to teach next.

TOPS modules are flexible. They can generally be scheduled in any order to meet your own class needs. Some lessons within certain modules, however, do require basic math skills or a knowledge of fundamental laboratory techniques. Review the task cards in this module now if you are not yet familiar with them. Decide whether you should teach any of these other TOPS modules first: *Measuring Length, Graphing, Metric Measure, Weighing* or *Electricity* (before *Magnetism*). It may be that your students already possess these requisite skills or that you can compensate with extra class discussion or special assistance.

☐ Number your task card masters in pencil.

The small number printed in the lower right corner of each task card shows its position within the overall series. If this ordering fits your schedule, copy each number into the blank parentheses directly above it at the top of the card. Be sure to use pencil rather than ink. You may decide to revise, upgrade or rearrange these task cards next time you teach this module. To do this, write your own better ideas on blank 4 x 6 index cards, and renumber them into the task card sequence wherever they fit best. In this manner, your curriculum will adapt and grow as you do.

☐ Copy your task card masters.

You have our permission to reproduce these task cards, for as long as you teach, with only 1 restriction: please limit the distribution of copies you make to the students you personally teach. Encourage other teachers who want to use this module to purchase their *own* copy. This supports TOPS financially, enabling us to continue publishing new TOPS modules for you. For a full list of task card options, please turn to the first task card masters numbered "cards 1-2."

☐ Collect needed materials.

Please see the opposite page.

☐ Organize a way to track completed assignment.

Keep write-ups on file in class. If you lack a vertical file, a box with a brick will serve. File folders or notebooks both make suitable assignment organizers. Students will feel a sense of accomplishment as they see their file folders grow heavy, or their notebooks fill up, with completed assignments. Easy reference and convenient review are assured, since all papers remain in one place.

Ask students to staple a sheet of numbered graph paper to the inside front cover of their file folder or notebook. Use this paper to track each student's progress through the module. Simply initial the corresponding task card number as students turn in each assignment.

☐ Review safety procedures.

Most TOPS experiments are safe even for small children. Certain lessons, however, require heat from a candle flame or Bunsen burner. Others require students to handle sharp objects like scissors, straight pins and razor blades. These task cards should not be attempted by immature students unless they are closely supervised. You might choose instead to turn these experiments into teacher demonstrations.

Unusual hazards are noted in the teaching notes and task cards where appropriate. But the curriculum cannot anticipate irresponsible behavior or negligence. It is ultimately the teacher's responsibility to see that common sense safety rules are followed at all times. Begin with these basic safety rules:

1. Eye Protection: Wear safety goggles when heating liquids or solids to high temperatures.
2. Poisons: Never taste anything unless told to do so.
3. Fire: Keep loose hair or clothing away from flames. Point test tubes which are heating away from your face and your neighbor's.
4. Glass Tubing: Don't force through stoppers. (The teacher should fit glass tubes to stoppers in advance, using a lubricant.)
5. Gas: Light the match first, before turning on the gas.

☐ Communicate your grading expectations.

Whatever your philosophy of grading, your students need to understand the standards you expect and how they will be assessed. Here is a grading scheme that counts individual effort, attitude and overall achievement. We think these 3 components deserve equal weight:

1. Pace (effort): Tally the number of check points you have initialed on the graph paper attached to each student's file folder or science notebook. Low ability students should be able to keep pace with gifted students, since write-ups are evaluated relative to individual performance standards. Students with absences or those who tend to work at a slow pace may (or may not) choose to overcome this disadvantage by assigning themselves more homework out of class.

2. Participation (attitude): This is a subjective grade assigned to reflect each student's attitude and class behavior. Active participators who work to capacity receive high marks. Inactive onlookers, who waste time in class and copy the results of others, receive low marks.

3. Exam (achievement): Task cards point toward generalizations that provide a base for hypothesizing and predicting. A final test over the entire module determines whether students understand relevant theory and can apply it in a predictive way.

Gathering Materials

Listed below is everything you'll need to teach this module. You already have many of these items. The rest are available from your supermarket, drugstore and hardware store. Laboratory supplies may be ordered through a science supply catalog. Hobby stores also carry basic science equipment.

Keep this classification key in mind as you review what's needed:

special in-a-box materials:	general on-the-shelf materials:
Italic type suggests that these materials are unusual. Keep these specialty items in a separate box. After you finish teaching this module, label the box for storage and put it away, ready to use again the next time you teach this module.	Normal type suggests that these materials are common. Keep these basics on shelves or in drawers that are readily accessible to your students. The next TOPS module you teach will likely utilize many of these same materials.
(substituted materials):	*optional materials:
A parentheses following any item suggests a ready substitute. These alternatives may work just as well as the original, perhaps better. Don't be afraid to improvise, to make do with what you have.	An asterisk sets these items apart. They are nice to have, but you can easily live without them. They are probably not worth the extra trip, unless you are gathering other materials as well.

Everything is listed in order of first use. Start gathering at the top of this list and work down. Ask students to bring recycled items from home. The teaching notes may occasionally suggest additional student activity under the heading "Extensions." Materials for these optional experiments are listed neither here nor in the teaching notes. Read the extension itself to find out what new materials, if any, are required.

Needed quantities depend on how many students you have, how you organize them into activity groups, and how you teach. Decide which of these 3 estimates best applies to you, then adjust quantities up or down as necessary:

$Q_1 / Q_2 / Q_3$
- **Single Student:** Enough for 1 student to do all the experiments.
- **Individualized Approach:** Enough for 30 students informally working in 10 lab groups, all self-paced.
- **Traditional Approach:** Enough for 30 students, organized into 10 lab groups, all doing the same lesson.

KEY:	*special in-a-box materials*	general on-the-shelf materials
	(substituted materials)	*optional materials

$Q_1 / Q_2 / Q_3$

1/1/1	box paper clips
1/10/10	scissors
1/10/10	*index cards
5/50/50	meters of adding machine tape
1/1/1	roll clear tape
1/20/20	meters of string
1/10/10	clean empty cans — 15 ounce size is best
1/1/1	roll masking tape
3/35/40	sheets notebook paper
1/2/5	*state road maps*
1/10/10	pennies
1/5/10	*calculators
1/10/10	*nuts and bolts — 5/8 inch size is best, about one inch long*
1/1/1	bottle white glue
1/5/10	straight pins
1/1/1	small piece aluminum foil

Sequencing Task Cards

This logic tree shows how all the task cards in this module tie together. In general, students begin at the trunk of the tree and work up through the related branches. As the diagram suggests, the way to upper level activities leads up from lower level activities.

At the teacher's discretion, certain activities can be omitted or sequences changed to meet specific class needs. The only activities that must be completed in sequence are indicated by leaves that open *vertically* into the ones above them. In these cases the lower activity is a prerequisite to the upper.

When possible, students should complete the task cards in the same sequence as numbered. If time is short, however, or certain students need to catch up, you can use the logic tree to identify concept-related *horizontal* activities. Some of these might be omitted since they serve only to reinforce learned concepts rather than introduce new ones.

On the other hand, if students complete all the activities at a certain horizontal concept level, then experience difficulty at the next higher level, you might go back down the logic tree to have students repeat specific key activities for greater reinforcement.

For whatever reason, when you wish to make sequence changes, you'll find this logic tree a valuable reference. Parentheses in the upper right corner of each task card allow you total flexibility. They are left blank so you can pencil in sequence numbers of your own choosing.

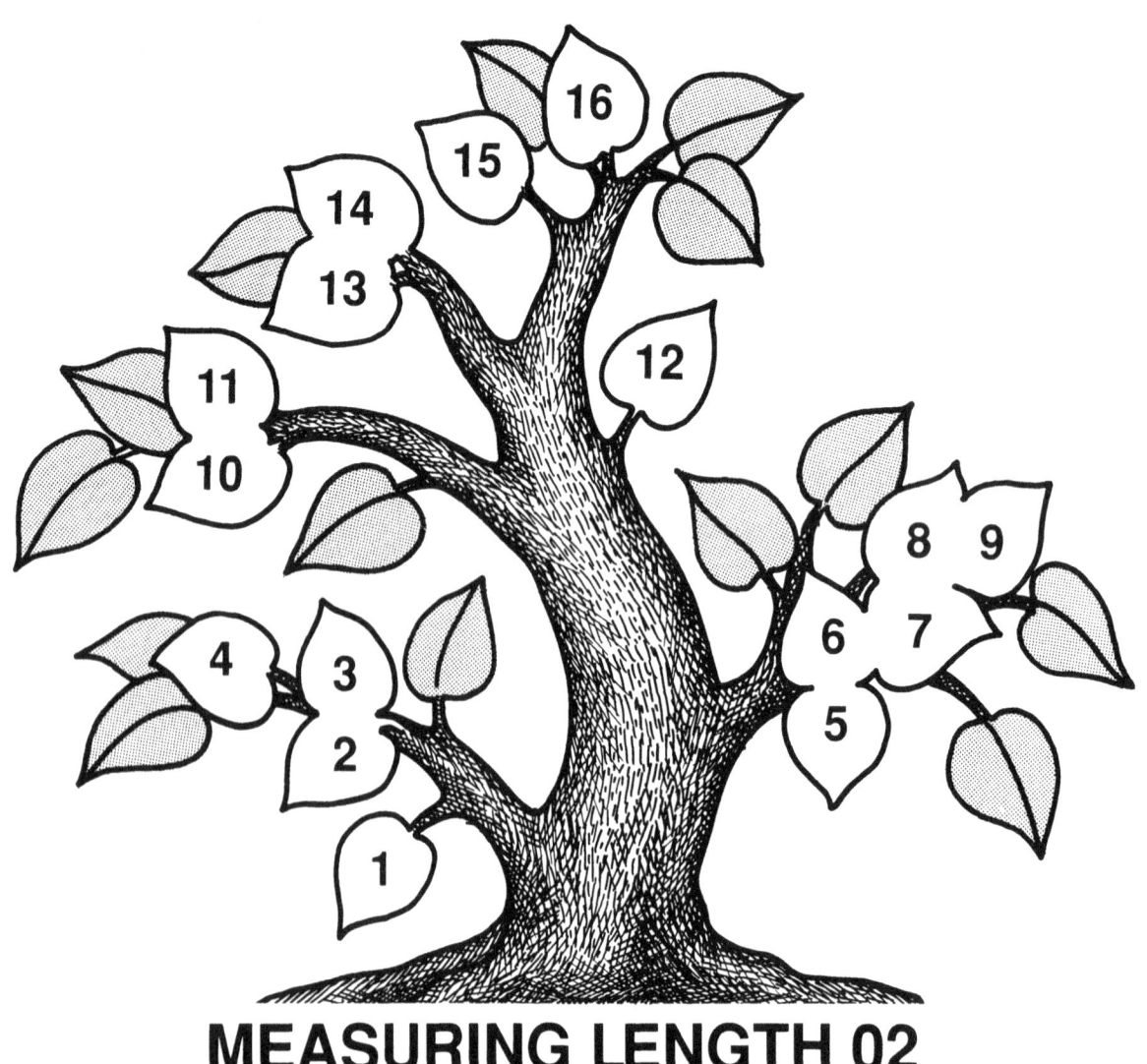

MEASURING LENGTH 02

LONG-RANGE OBJECTIVES

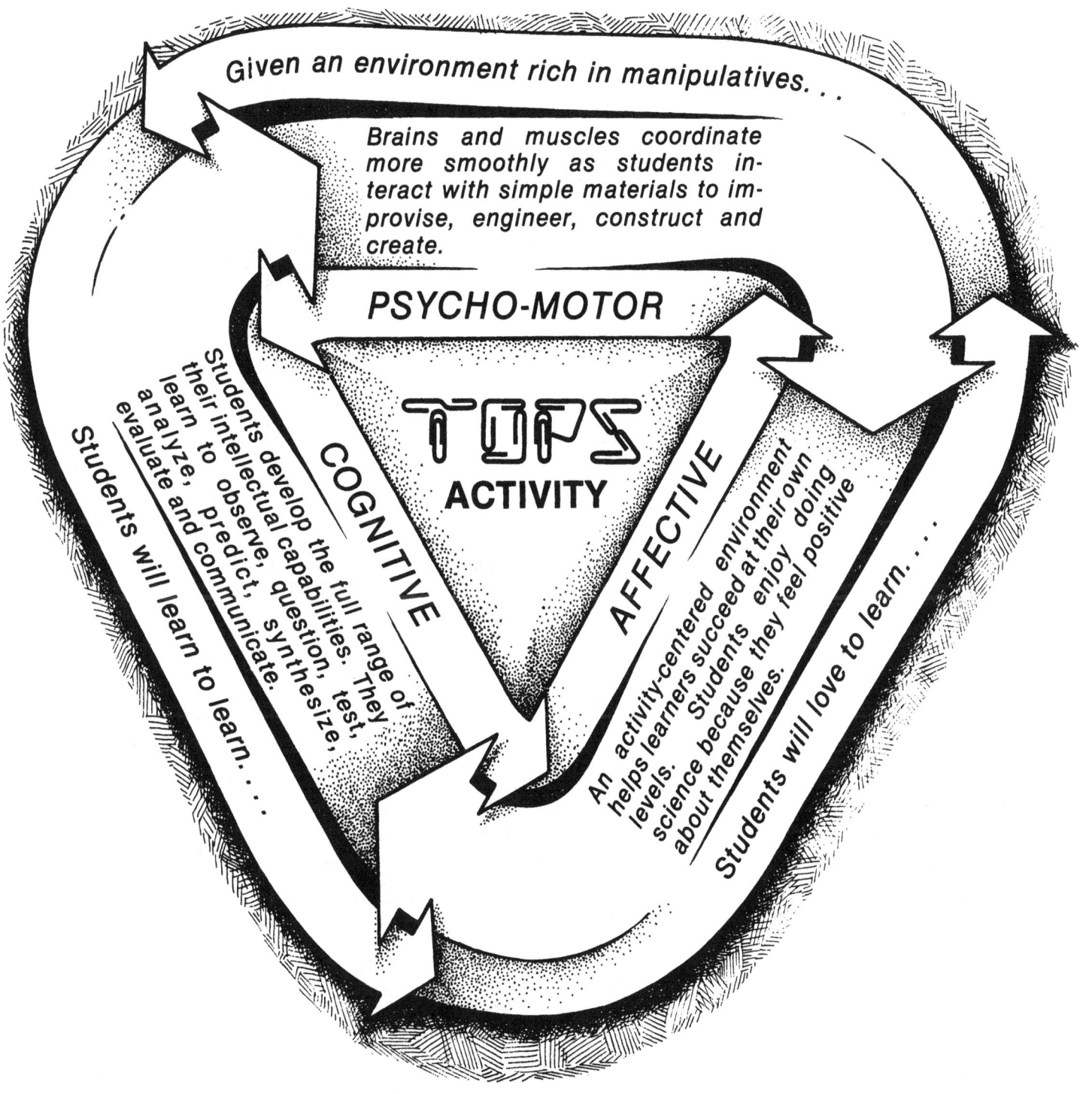

Review / Test Questions

Photocopy the questions below. On a separate sheet of blank paper, cut and paste those boxes you want to use as test questions. Include questions of your own design, as well. Crowd all these questions onto a single page for students to answer on another paper, or leave space for student responses after each question, as you wish. Duplicate a class set and your custom-made test is ready to use. Use leftover questions as a review in preparation for the final exam.

task 1
Two students walk the length of a field to measure its length. One measures 71 paces; the other 82 paces.
a. Why does each student get a different answer?
b. Describe a better way to measure the field.

task 1-2
This line is 1 unit long.
———
a. Draw a line that is 1 deka-unit long.
b. Draw a line that is 3 deci-units long.
c. Is the top of your test paper wider than 1,000 centi-units?

task 2
A yard is 36 inches long. How long is...
  a. 1 centi-yard?
  b. 1 milli-yard?
  c. 1 kilo-yard?

task 2, 4
Is a kilo-yard longer than a mile? Explain.

task 3
Balance each equation with the correct number.
a. 1 meter = ? cm   d. 2 km = ? m
b. 5 cm = ? mm   e. 50 m = ? dkm
c. 20 mm = ? cm   f. 30 cm = ? dm

task 3, 4
Roughly estimate each distance using the most appropriate units of measure — mm, cm, m or km.
a. Height of your room.
b. Four times round the school track.
c. Length of your little finger.
d. Thickness of 2 pennies.

task 4
Add *equal*, *greater than*, or *less than* symbols between each set of numbers to make each statement true.
a. 2 km ? 1 mi   d. 100 mi ? 160 k
b. 5 mi ? 8 km   e. 1.6 mi ? 1 k
c. 10 km ? 16 mi   f. 40 km ? 25 mi

task 5-6
Summarize the rules for measuring in significant figures.

task 5-9 A
Two students correctly measure the diameter of a nickle as 2.14 cm and 2.15 cm respectively. Explain why they get different answers.

task 5-9 B
Two scientists correctly measure the length of the same pencil as 14.65 cm and 14.7 cm. Describe the calibrations that are on each of their rulers.

task 5-9 C
Write each measure in significant cm.
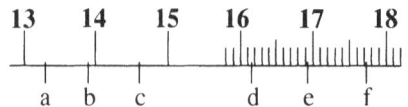

task 5-9 D
Write each measure in significant cm.
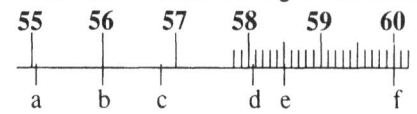

task 5-9 E
a. Use this ruler to measure the length of a paper clip in significant figures.

b. Use this ruler to measure the diameter of a penny in significant figures.
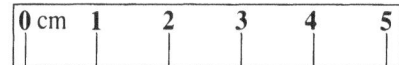

task 10-11
a. Use just a single paper clip to measure the length of this test paper in paper clips. Estimate your uncertainty as a plus or minus figure.
b. How might you check whether your uncertainty is reasonable?

task 10-11
A student with feet that each measure 20.0 ± .3 cm paces off exactly 100 steps heel to toe.
a. How far did he travel in cm? Include measuring uncertainty in your answer.
b. How far did he travel in meters?

task 12
Explain how you would use a bicycle to accurately measure the length of a field in meters.

task 12
The diameter of a car tire measures .7 meters.
a. Find its circumference.
b. How far does it travel in 100 revolutions? Show your work.

task 13-14
Fold this test paper along the dashed line to make a small metric ruler.
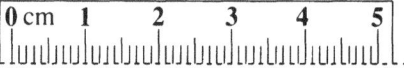
Use it to measure the thickness of a leaf in your textbook to an accuracy of .001 mm. Show your work.

task 13-14
A disk with a 10 cm circumference moves up or down a threaded bolt at 1 revolution per millimeter.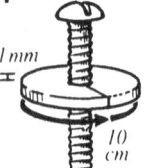
When measuring with this instrument, should you report the thickness of a nickle as 1.9 mm, 1.93 mm, 1.931 mm, or 1.9306 mm? Explain.

task 15
Finish this equation to find the number of cm in 3 km: $\frac{3 \text{ km}}{1} \times$ _____

task 3, 15
a. A standard-sized paper clip is very close to 1 mm thick. Use it to draw a decimeter ruler to scale. Show all millimeter divisions in the first centimeter only.
b. Use unit analysis to show how many clips would stack 1 km high.

task 12, 16
A student measures a meter stick to be 99.5 cm long. Compute her percent error.

task 16
Your climbing party wishes to practice rappelling down a cliff face (lowering oneself on a rope). You need at least twice as much rope as the distance you'll drop. How can you be sure you have enough?

Copyright © 1991 by TOPS Learning Systems.

Answers

task 1
a. Different measurements result because the students are using different standards of measure. Their feet have different lengths.
b. Measure the field with an accepted standard of measure, a meter tape, for example.

task 1-2
a. *Students should draw a line 10 times as long.*
b. *Students should draw a line 3/10 as long:* —
c. A thousand centi-units equals 10 units:
$$1000 \times \frac{1}{100} \text{ units} = 10 \text{ units}$$
This distance (equal to the deka-unit drawn in part a), is less than the width of the test paper.

task 2
a. 1 centi-yard = .36 inches
b. 1 milli-yard = .036 inches
c. 1 kilo-yard = 1,000 yards
        (36,000 inches)

task 2, 4
No. There are 5,280 feet in a mile, or 1,760 yards. But there are only 1,000 yards in a kilo-yard.

task 3
a. 1 m = 100 cm   d. 2 km = 2,000 m
b. 5 cm = 50 mm   e. 50 m = 5 dkm
c. 20 mm = 2 cm   f. 30 cm = 3 dm

task 3, 4
a. 3 m   c. 5 cm
b. 1.6 km   d. 3 mm

task 4
a. 2 km > 1 mi   d. 100 mi = 160 k
b. 5 mi = 8 km   e. 1.6 mi > 1 k
c. 10 km < 16 mi   f. 40 km = 25 mi

task 5-6
Write down all the decimal places you are sure about, then estimate between the lines to get the last number. If the measurement hits a line, make the last estimated digit zero.

task 5-9 A
The students get different answers because the last digit is estimated and therefore uncertain.

task 5-9 B
The scientist who measured a length of 14.65 cm estimated between mm calibrations on the ruler to an uncertain hundredth cm. The scientist who measured a length of 14.7 cm estimated between cm calibrations on the ruler to an uncertain tenth cm.

task 5-9 C
a. 13.3 cm   d. 16.17 cm
b. 13.9 cm   e. 16.92 cm
c. 14.6 cm   f. 17.72 cm

task 5-9 D
a. 55.1 cm   d. 58.08 cm
b. 56.0 cm   e. 58.50 cm
c. 56.7 cm   f. 60.00 cm

task 5-9 E
a. length of paper clip = 3.25 cm
b. diameter of penny = 1.9 cm

task 10-11
These answers are based on a standard 8.5 x 11 inch sheet of paper.
a. paper length = 8.7 ± .2 clips
b. Measure the length of the paper several times and observe the variation in your answer. Better yet, compare your answer with other class members to see if most measurements fall within your estimated margin of error.

task 10-11
a. $\frac{20.0 \pm .3 \text{ cm}}{\text{step}} \times 100 \text{ steps} = 2000 \pm 30 \text{ cm}$
b. 20 ± .3 m

task 12
First find the circumference of the bicycle tire, either by measuring it with a meter tape directly, or by measuring the diameter and multiplying by π. Then mark the tire with something easy to see, so you can count the number of revolutions it makes as you push it across the field. Multiply the tire's circumference by its total number of revolutions to compute the distance.

task 12
a. C = πd = 3.14 x .7 m = 2.2 m
b. $\frac{2.2 \text{ m}}{1 \text{ rev}} \times 100 \text{ rev} = 220 \text{ m}$

task 13-14
To obtain this degree of accuracy, students should measure 100 textbook leaves, then divide by 100:
    100 leaves = 6.6 mm
    1 leaf = .066 mm

task 13-14
If a full turn of 10 cm moves the disk up or down just 1 mm, then a...
  1 cm turn moves it .1 mm
  .1 cm turn moves it .01 mm
  .01 cm turn moves it .001 mm.
The disk cannot be read with greater certainty than this, so the thickness of the nickle cannot be known with greater accuracy than 1.931 mm.

task 15
$$\frac{3 \text{ km}}{1} \times \frac{1,000 \text{ m}}{1 \text{ km}} \times \frac{100 \text{ cm}}{1 \text{ m}} = 300,000 \text{ cm}$$

task 3, 15
a.
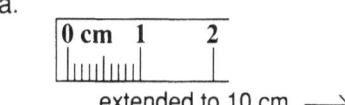
    extended to 10 cm ⟶
b.
$$\frac{1 \text{ km}}{1} \times \frac{1,000 \text{ m}}{1 \text{ km}} \times \frac{1,000 \text{ mm}}{1 \text{ m}} \times \frac{1 \text{ clip}}{1 \text{ mm}} = 1,000,000 \text{ clips}$$

task 12, 16
% error = $\frac{.5 \text{ cm}}{100 \text{ cm}} \times 100 = .5\%$

task 16
Stretch out the rope along the bottom of the cliff. Fold it to reach half its total length. Then stand back so your outstretched hand span just takes in the height of the cliff. If you now turn your hand along the horizontal, your fingers should not appear to reach to the end of your doubled rope.

TEACHING NOTES
For Activities 1-16

Task Objective (TO) measure length with thumb widths, paper clips and centimeters. To evaluate each unit as a measuring standard.

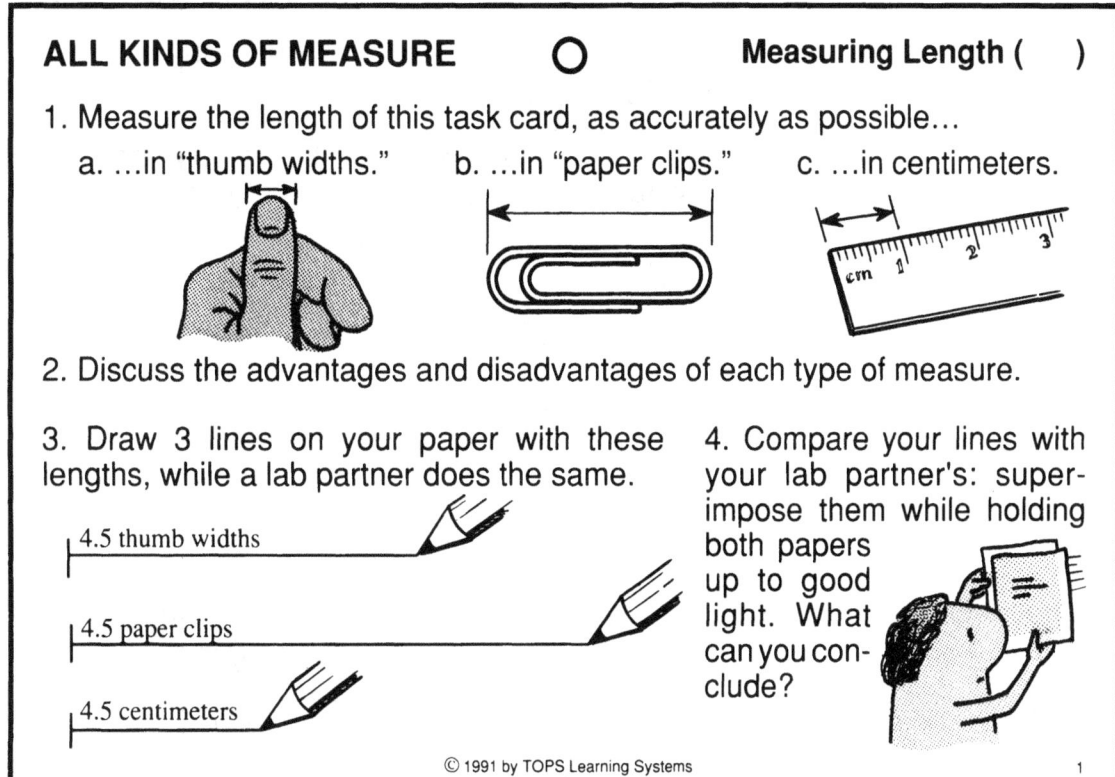

Answers / Notes

1a. length = 8 1/2 thumb widths   1b. length = 4 2/3 paper clips   1c. length = 15.25 centimeters

2. Thumb widths are a convenient unit of measure because you always have them right at hand. But thumb size varies from person to person. It is not a standard unit of measure.

Paper clips are also convenient. If there is just a single brand of clips circulating in your classroom, then everyone would measure the card using the same standard. The size of the paper clip is not universally agreed upon, however. People in other places likely use other brands that are larger or smaller than this class standard.

Centimeters are the best unit of measure to use because their size is agreed upon around the world. A centimeter ruler used by a scientist in Egypt, for example, is exactly the same size as a centimeter ruler in Canada.

3.
                      4.5 thumb widths
              4.5 paper clips
                      4.5 centimeters

4. Lines measured in thumb widths likely show the widest variation, since this is a non-standard unit.

Lines measured in paper clips may show variation as well, because errors accumulate as the paper clip is placed end to end. *(If both students use a chained paper clip ruler, however, line lengths will be much closer.)*

Lines measured in centimeters should nearly match if they are carefully drawn, since everyone is using a common measuring standard.

Materials

☐ Paper clips. Students may choose to lay just 1 clip end to end, or chain several together.
☐ A centimeter ruler. Supply commercial metric rulers. Or photocopy the supplementary page at the back of this book — one sheet for every two students. Direct them to carefully cut out the 20-cm ruler. No white space should remain as a border under the mm subdivisions.
☐ Scissors for cutting out the cm ruler.
☐ A straight edge. An index card or ruler will serve.

(TO) define the decimal equivalents of metric prefixes, and use them in combination with other units of measure.

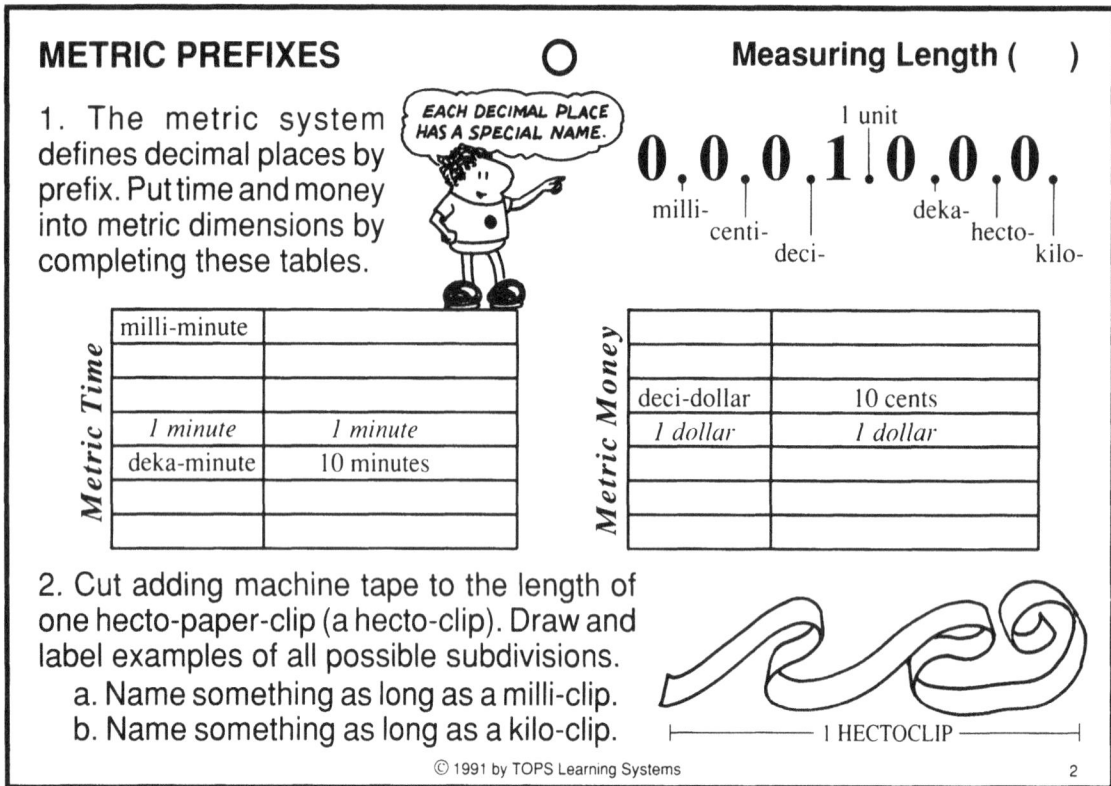

Answers / Notes

1.

Metric Time		
	milli-minute	.06 seconds
	centi-minute	.6 seconds
	deci-minute	6 seconds
	1 minute	*1 minute*
	deka-minute	10 minutes
	hecto-minute	100 minutes
	kilo-minute	1,000 minutes

Metric Money		
	milli-dollar	.1 cent
	centi-dollar	1 cent
	deci-dollar	10 cents
	1 dollar	*1 dollar*
	deka-dollar	10 dollars
	hecto-dollar	100 dollars
	kilo-dollar	1,000 dollars

2. *Students need not mark all 100 paper clip divisions. Once a length of 10 clips (a deka-clip) is established, the strip can be folded at 10 successive deka-clip intervals to find the length of the whole hecto-clip. All intervals except the milli-clip and kilo-clip can be represented. The centi-clip is about as thick as thread.*

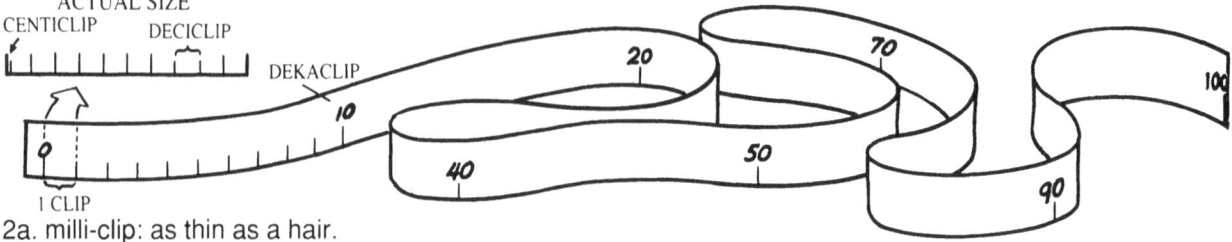

2a. milli-clip: as thin as a hair.
2b. kilo-clip: as long as the length of a room. *(This is about 33 meters or 100 feet.)*

Materials

☐ Adding machine tape. Precut strips about 3.5 meters long.
☐ Scissors.
☐ A paper clip.

(TO) get acquainted with meters, centimeters, and millimeters. To make an accurate meter tape to use in later activities.

METRIC EQUIVALENTS   Measuring Length (   )

1. Carefully cut out a ten-centimeter ruler. No white edge should remain under the small divisions.

2. Use adding machine tape to extend this ruler to one meter. Accurately mark *all* centimeter divisions with the other 20-cm ruler, then number every 5 divisions.

3. Using your ruler as a reference, complete these qualitative and quantitative metric tables. (Label and save your tape for later activities.)

Qualitative

millimeter	
meter	as wide as a doorway

Quantitative

1 dm	1/10 meter (.1 m)
1 m	1 meter (1 m)

4. Complete each equation:

1 cm = ? mm   1 m = ? cm   1 m = ? mm   1 km = ? m
1 mm = ? cm   1 cm = ? m   1 mm = ? m   1 m = ? km

© 1991 by TOPS Learning Systems

Introduction

Copy this table on your blackboard, but don't fill in either column. Within the context of a class discussion, ask volunteers to think of common distances appropriate to each measure. Keep a meter stick or improvised tape handy to use as a reference.

millimeters	7 mm	as thick as a pencil
centimeters	18 cm	a long as a new pencil
decimeters	8 dm	as wide as your desk
meters	2 m	as tall as an adult
dekameters	1 dkm	a long parking space
hectometers	4 hm	once around the track
kilometers	1.6 km	about a mile

Answers / Notes

3.

Qualitative

millimeter	as thick as a paper clip
centimeter	a little wider than a paper clip
decimeter	as tall as this task card
meter	as wide as a doorway
dekameter	as long as a classroom
hectometer	as long as a football field
kilometer	about a 10 minute walk

Quantitative

1 mm	1/1,000 meter (.001 m)
1 cm	1/100 meter (.01 m)
1 dm	1/10 meter (.1 m)
1 m	1 meter (1 m)
1 dkm	10 meter (10 m)
1 hm	100 meter (100 m)
1 km	1,000 meter (1,000 m)

4. 1 cm = 10 mm   1 m = 100 cm   1 m = 1,000 mm   1 km = 1,000 m
    1 mm = .1 cm   1 cm = .01 m   1 mm = .001 m   1 m = .001 km

Materials

☐ Paper rulers, 10 and 20 centimeters long. Photocopy these from the supplementary page at the back of the book — one sheet for every two students. These rulers will be used throughout this module. Ask students to save them.
☐ Scissors.
☐ Clear tape.
☐ Adding machine tape. Precut strips a little longer than a meter.

(TO) compare the length of a kilometer with the length of a mile.

MILES AND KILOMETERS   **Measuring Length ( )**

1. Cut out a 6 inch ruler (1/2 foot). Use it to cut exactly one *milli*-mile of string. Explain how you did this.

2. Your milli-mile string is what fraction of a mile? Your meter tape is what fraction of a kilometer?

3. Your milli-mile string and meter tape are equally scaled-down versions of a full mile and a full kilometer.
   a. Which is longer, a kilometer or a mile?
   b. How many times does the shorter fit into the longer? (Round off to 2 digits.)

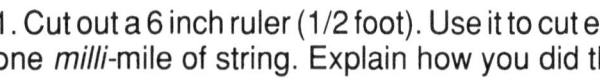

4. Complete this conversion table.

5. A highway speed limit is 60 mph. Convert this to kph.

MILE	KILOMETER
1	
10	
	8
	160

© 1991 by TOPS Learning Systems

Answers / Notes

1. There are 5,280 feet in 1 mile. A thousandth of this distance, 1 milli-mile, must therefore equal 5.280 feet, just over 5 1/4 feet or 10 1/2 rulers: 5.280 feet = 5 feet + .280 feet
= 10 rulers + (.28)(12 inches)
= 10 rulers + 3.36 inches

A convenient way to measure this much string is to tape the 6-inch ruler to the table top, then pass measured segments of string above it.

2. One milli-mile = 1/1,000 of a mile; one meter = 1/1,000 of a kilometer.

3a. A mile is longer than a kilometer.

3b. The scaled-down kilometer fits into the scaled-down mile 1.61 times. Rounded to 2 digits, 1.6 kilometers equals 1 mile.

4.

MILE	KILOMETER
1	1.6
10	16
5	8
100	160

5. 60 mph × $\frac{1.6 \text{ kph}}{1 \text{ mph}}$ = 96 kph ≈ 100 kph

Materials

☐ A foot ruler with inches divided into tenths. Photocopy this from the supplementary page at the back of this book.
☐ Scissors.
☐ String.
☐ The meter tape constructed previously.

(**TO**) learn how to read a ruler accurately by estimating the last digit.

ESTIMATE THE LAST DIGIT ○   Measuring Length ( )

1. Write the correct measure for each letter. Always make the last digit zero when the hairline hits the mark dead center.

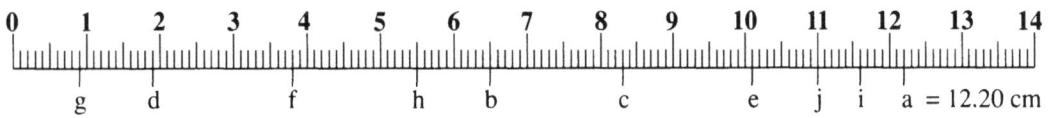

2. Write the correct measure. Estimate between marks when the hairline doesn't hit dead center. If it does, make the last digit zero.

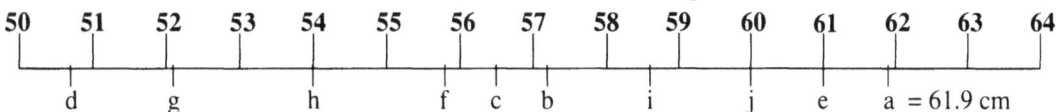

3. Write the correct measure. Apply the rules you learned above when writing the last digit.

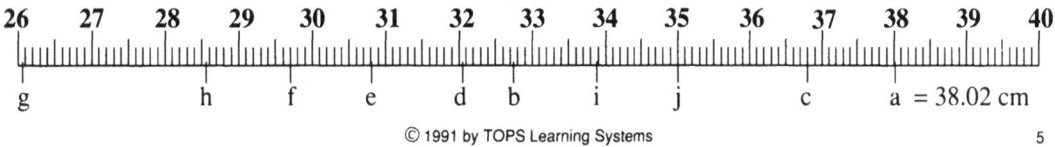

© 1991 by TOPS Learning Systems

Introduction

Draw larger-than-scale versions of centimeter rulers A and B on your blackboard as shown. Make them big enough to be easily seen from the back of your room, taking care to leave equal space between your subdivisions. Randomly tape a piece of string over the rulers, weighted by a paper clip or two to keep it straight.

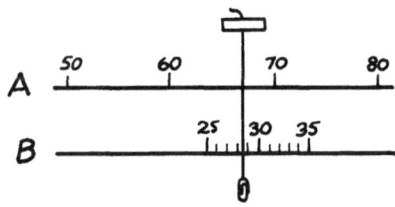

Use this prop to teach your class about accurate measurements. Begin with the A scale, asking students where the string crosses the line. Take an opinion ballot if time allows. Emphasize how there is agreement about all certain figures (unless someone makes an error), but that the last digit between the line is estimated, and therefore open to debate. Focus attention on the B scale next. Notice that it can be read to 3 significant figures instead of 2.

Continue with new string positions, including one where the string hits a line dead center so that the last estimated digit is zero.

Answers / Notes

1-3. Insist that students get into the good habit of writing units with each answer.

1.	2.	3.
a = 12.20 cm	a = 61.9 cm	a = 38.02 cm
b = 6.50 cm	b = 57.2 cm	b = 32.74 cm
c = 8.30 cm	c = 56.5 cm	c = 36.80 cm
d = 1.90 cm	d = 50.7 cm	d = 32.05 cm
e = 10.10 cm	e = 61.0 cm	e = 30.81 cm
f = 3.80 cm	f = 55.8 cm	f = 29.70 cm
g = 0.90 cm	g = 52.1 cm	g = 26.08 cm
h = 5.50 cm	h = 54.0 cm	h = 28.57 cm
i = 11.60 cm	i = 58.6 cm	i = 33.88 cm
j = 11.00 cm	j = 60.0 cm	j = 35.00 cm

There may be differences in the last digit, which is estimated.

Materials
None.

(TO) distinguish between certain figures and uncertain figures. To appreciate that no measurement is exact.

SIGNIFICANT FIGURES ○ Measuring Length ( )

1. The last digit in any good measurement is estimated, and therefore uncertain. Write *two* possible measurements for each letter.

a.
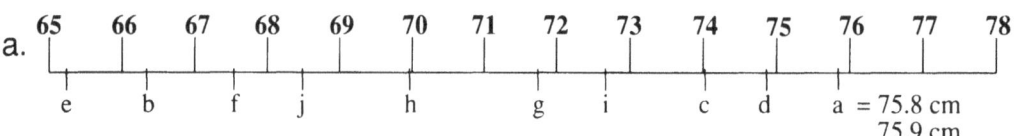
a = 75.8 cm
75.9 cm

b.

a = 49.16 cm
49.17 cm

2. Five students gave these measurements for letter "e" above: 40.36 cm, 43.60 cm, 40.37 cm, 40.36 cm, 40.35 cm. Are all these measurements valid? Explain.

3. Any valid measurement contains only significant figures. What are significant figures?

4. Is it possible to calibrate a ruler so accurately that measuring uncertainty is eliminated? Explain.

© 1991 by TOPS Learning Systems

Answers / Notes

1a.	1b.
a = 75.8 cm or 75.9 cm	a = 49.16 cm or 49.17 cm
b = 66.3 cm or 66.4 cm	b = 41.18 cm or 41.19 cm
c = 74.0 cm or 74.1 cm	c = 47.69 cm or 47.70 cm
d = 74.8 cm or 74.9 cm	d = 45.73 cm or 45.74 cm
e = 65.2 cm or 65.3 cm	e = 40.36 cm or 40.37 cm
f = 67.5 cm or 67.6 cm	f = 38.41 cm or 38.42 cm
g = 71.7 cm or 71.8 cm	g = 46.72 cm or 46.73 cm
h = 69.9 cm or 70.0 cm	h = 39.56 cm or 39.57 cm
i = 72.6 cm or 72.7 cm	i = 42.75 cm or 42.76 cm
j = 68.4 cm or 68.5 cm	j = 44.31 cm or 44.32 cm

Expect answers to differ from these by ± .02 cm.

2. Letter "e" lies between 40.3 cm and 40.4 cm. This makes digits "four," "zero" and "three" certain beyond dispute. The second measurement is invalid because its first 3 figures are different than these. The other 4 measurements are all valid because there is disagreement only in the last estimated digit.

3. Significant figures are all the numbers you are certain about in a measurement, plus 1 last estimated digit.

4. No. Even if you subdivide the ruler with very narrow divisions, until they almost touch each other, there is still uncertainty in the narrow slivers of space left in between.

Materials

None.

(TO) practice reading metric scales calibrated in centimeters and millimeters.

HAIRLINE MEASURE **Measuring Length (   )**

1. Cut out the ruled rectangle on the dashed line. Wrap it around a can, taping the ends to the metal surface with 1 long piece of tape.

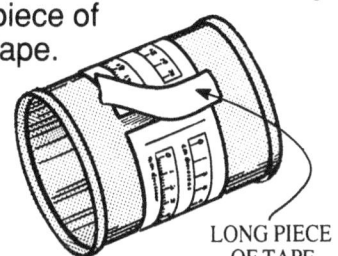

2. Cut out a 4 cm x 26 cm band of waxed paper and wrap it very *snugly* over the rectangle. Tape it to itself so the band remains free to slide.

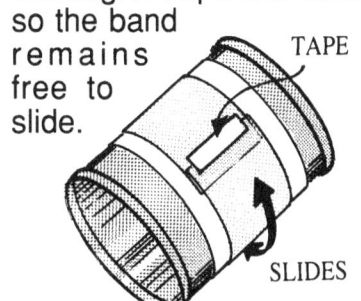

3. Tape a dark strand of straight hair across the waxed band. Line it up with the vertical line at the beginning of the rulers.

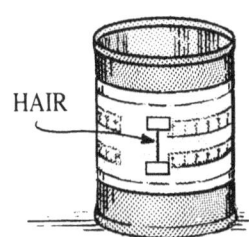

4. Move your hairline along the *lower* mm divisions, stopping at these intervals. Describe your trip.
   a. 12.00, 12.10, 12.20, 12.30, 12.40, 12.50, 12.60, ..., 13.00.
   b. 12.00, 12.01, 12.02, 12.03, 12.04, 12.05, 12.06, ..., 12.10.

5. Repeat your journey of 4a and 4b along the *upper* cm divisions.

© 1991 by TOPS Learning Systems

Answers / Notes

1. *Students should work in pairs, both here and in the next few activities. They need only 1 can between them.*
   The whole seam should by taped. This firmly attaches the rulers to the can, and prevents the seam in the overlaid waxed paper (applied in step 2) from snagging on any raised edges as it slides over this joint.

2. *The waxed paper must be taped tightly enough to remain firmly in place when it is not intentionally moved.*

3. *Tape should not extend over the edge of the waxed paper to the rulered paper behind. This waxed paper must remain free to slide around the can.*

4a. The hairline moves in 1 mm increments, stopping at each division on the ruler over a distance of 1 cm.

4b. The hairline just barely moves in .1 mm increments, stopping at estimated intervals between a 1-mm subdivision.

5a. The hairline moves in 1 mm increments stopping at estimated intervals between a 1-cm subdivision.

5b. This is a small, difficult journey. The hairline just barely moves in .1 mm increments, stopping at estimated intervals over a 1 mm distance that is also estimated.

Materials

☐ A rectangle containing cm and mm rulers. Photocopy this from the supplementary page at the back of this book.
☐ Scissors.
☐ A clean, empty tin can with its label removed. A 15 ounce olive or vegetable can is the ideal size. If you substitute a smaller soup-can size, you'll need to trim back the ruler rectangle in step 1 (on the high end of the rulers) so it doesn't quite overlap. If you substitute a large juice-can size, you'll need to increase the length of the waxed paper in step 2 so that it overlaps itself.
☐ A strand of straight dark hair. Thread may be substituted, but it makes a less accurate hairline.
☐ Tape. The position of the hair between pieces of tape is best defined by easy-to-see masking tape.

(TO) agree with a friend, within acceptable limits of uncertainty, where the hairline crosses a scale.

AGREE / DISAGREE (1) ○   Measuring Length (   )

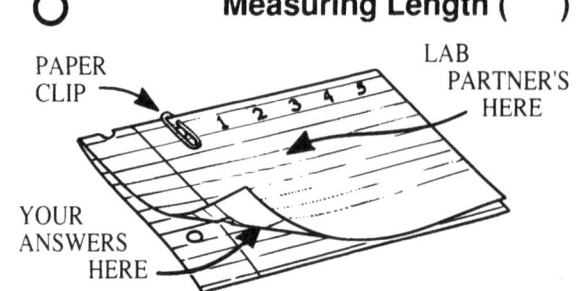

1. Work with a lab partner. Fold a clean sheet of notebook paper in half. Number along the fold, and paper clip as shown.

2. Play agree / disagree on the *upper* cm divisions of your can.

    a. DIAL any random measure without looking at the hairline.
    b. WRITE the hairline measurement in significant figures. You use the *inside* of the paper, while your lab partner writes an independent answer on the *outside*.
    c. COMPARE answers inside and out. Advance the paper clip by 1 number if you agree (estimated digit off by no more than one). Slide back 2 numbers if you disagree (estimated digit off by more than one, or certain digits disagree). Play until you reach 5.

3. Repeat this game on the *lower* mm divisions of your can.

4. Which scale is hardest to play? Why?

© 1991 by TOPS Learning Systems   8

Answers / Notes

2-3. *This game is cooperative. If both players write answers that agree, they advance 1 space. For example, 13.9 cm agrees with 13.8 cm because the last estimated digit differs by no more than 1. (Notice that 13.9 cm also agrees with 14.0 cm. Again the last estimated digit differs by no more than 1, even though the units place must change.) Answers that differ by more than this are penalized: slide the paper clip back 2 spaces, but no lower than zero.*

4. The lower scale is much harder to play, because the estimated interval is only 1 mm wide, not 1 cm wide like the scale above. If players differ by more than a hundredth, they must slide the paper clip back 2 spaces.

Materials

☐ The hairline measuring can constructed in the previous activity.
☐ A paper clip.
☐ A sheet of notebook paper.

(TO) practice measuring line lengths in significant figures with centimeter and millimeter rulers. To estimate uncertainty as a plus-or-minus figure.

AGREE / DISAGREE (2) ○ Measuring Length ( )

1. Fold, number and paper clip a clean sheet of notebook paper from 0 to 5 as before. Use a 20 cm paper ruler to play another game of agree / disagree: MEASURE each line independently; COMPARE answers; SLIDE the paper clip forward or back, following previous rules.

  a. Is the game easier to play with a ruler or with a hairline? Explain.
  b. How would you revise the game rules to make it easier to win?

2. Uncertainty in a measurement can be expressed as "plus or minus." The length of line m (the bottom line) expressed in this way is 9.91 ± .01 cm.
  a. List 3 possible line lengths given by this number.
  b. Does 9.92 ± .01 cm agree with 9.90 ± .01 cm? Explain.
  c. Try another game, writing measurements with an uncertainty (± .01).

© 1991 by TOPS Learning Systems

Answers / Notes

1. *Students should measure one line at a time, comparing their answers before proceeding to the next line. Because measurements can differ by no more than .01 mm, it is difficult to agree. Many students may give up before winning the game.*

1a. *This game is more difficult to play with a ruler than with a hairline. The ruler must be aligned at the zero end before reading the length of each line. This is an important source of error not present when reading a hairline.*

1b. *To make winning more attainable, increase the tolerance of allowed uncertainty to .02 mm (certainly not more than .03 mm).*

2. *Your photocopier may not faithfully reproduce at exactly 100%. Minor size distortions can occur along the width or length of your copies, or in both directions, even though the machine is set for actual-size reproductions. So measure line m yourself, with a ruler reproduced on your own copier. If it doesn't measure 9.91±.01 cm, change the task card numbers to match your different result.*

2a. 9.90 cm, 9.91 cm, 9.92 cm

2b. Yes. Both measures share a common value, 9.91 cm.

2c. *The allowed tolerance is doubled from step 1. Now the game is relatively easy to win.*

Materials
- A paper clip.
- A sheet of notebook paper.
- A 20 cm paper ruler.

(TO) determine how specific body measurements conform to general body proportion equations. To work with measuring uncertainty.

NORM AVERAGE ○ **Measuring Length (   )**

1. Work with a lab partner to measure each length 3 times in significant figures. (Don't let the results of one trial influence your measurement in the next.) Use these trials to estimate the uncertainty in each measurement.

	trial 1	trial 2	trial 3	average ± uncertainty
fathom				
height				
forearm				
foot				
span				

2. These equations fit the body proportions of Norm Average. How well do they fit you? (Note: In part c, multiplying a measurement also multiplies its uncertainty.)
   a. fathom = height   b. forearm = foot   c. 8 spans = fathom

© 1991 by TOPS Learning Systems

Answers / Notes

1. *Uncertainty varies from body part to body part. Height, for example, can be measured quite precisely using a level book to project the end point to a wall, and a piece of masking tape to mark it. The forearm, by contrast, has indefinite end points at the wrist and elbow, creating greater uncertainty. Measuring uncertainty in a fathom is even greater, depending on how far you stretch. Expect a range of uncertainties, from a minimum of ±.1 cm to a maximum of ±1 cm. Here is a sample result:*

	trial 1	trial 2	trial 3	average ± uncertainty
fathom	161.8 cm	161.3 cm	160.0 cm	161 ± 1 cm
height	165.6 cm	165.9 cm	165.8 cm	165.8 ± .2 cm
forearm	22.6 cm	22.9 cm	22.2 cm	22.5 ± .5 cm
foot	22.4 cm	21.9 cm	22.1 cm	22.1 ± .3 cm
span	20.0 cm	20.0 cm	20.1 cm	20.0 ± .1 cm

2a. fathom ≠ height: Using the longest possible fathom (162 cm) and the shortest possible height (165.6 cm), there is still a difference of 3.6 cm.
2b. forearm = foot: The forearm and foot are equal within a range of 22.0 cm to 22.4 cm.
2c. 8 spans = fathom: Multiplying the span and its uncertainty by 8 yields 160 ± .8 cm. This equals a fathom (161 ± 1 cm) within a range of 160.0 cm to 160.8 cm.

Materials

☐ An improvised meter tape.
☐ A wall to stand against for measuring height, plus masking tape and a book.

(TO) practice measuring lengths of different magnitude. To estimate uncertainty.

LONG AND SHORT　　○　　　　**Measuring Length ( )**

1. Find each measure below. Be sure to:
   ...use the best unit (mm, cm, m or km).
   ...express each measure in significant figures.
   ...estimate uncertainty using plus-or-minus notation.

| a. Width of a sheet of notebook paper. | b. Distance from your school to the state capitol building. | c. Length of your classroom. | d. Thickness of a penny. |

 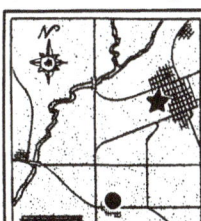 

2. Justify your uncertainty for each measure above. Explain why you chose the numbers you did.

3. Can you think of ways to reduce the uncertainty in any of these measures? Explain.

© 1991 by TOPS Learning Systems

Answers / Notes

1. *Answers may vary from these, but should remain internally consistent for your particular class.*
   - 1a. 21.71 ± .03 cm
   - 1b. 45 ± 5 km
   - 1c. 12.32 ± .04 m
   - 1d. 1.2 ± .2 mm

2a. In activity 9, measuring uncertainty for the 20-cm ruler was estimated to be ±.01 cm. This error increases to perhaps ±.03 cm because the ruler must be used twice to span the paper.

2b. The distance from any location on the map to the center of the capitol city is known to perhaps ±1 km. But considerable uncertainty must be added in estimating the distance from school house to capital building.

2c. There is perhaps ±.3 cm of uncertainty as the meter tape is laid end to end. This error arises from not keeping the ruler going in a straight line, not meeting exactly end to end, and internal measuring error in the ruler. Since the ruler was used 12 times across the room, this error multiplies to ±3.6 cm or roughly ±.04 m.

2d. The 20-cm ruler is certain to ±.01 cm or ±.1 mm. But there appears to be considerable variation in the thickness of even a single penny. So the uncertainty was doubled to .2 mm.

3. *Students may not think of a different method for all categories.*

3a. Use a magnifying glass to enlarge your viewing area.

3b. Drive the distance from your school to the steps of the capitol building, noting the starting and ending distances on your odometer.

3c. Use a long commercial meter tape that you don't have to lay end to end.

3d. Measure the height of a stack of 100 pennies, then divide by 100.

Materials

- ☐ An improvised meter tape.
- ☐ A piece of notebook paper.
- ☐ A 20 cm metric ruler.
- ☐ A state map.
- ☐ A penny.

(TO) measure length using a rolling can. To estimate uncertainty.

ROLLING MEASURE O   **Measuring Length (   )**

1. Get an empty can. Call its diameter "d" and its circumference "C."

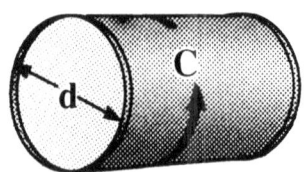

a. Measure d with your meter tape to an accuracy of 0.1 cm. Why can't you be more accurate than this?

b. Calculate C using this formula:
$C = \pi d = 3.14\, d$

c. Now measure C with your meter tape. Compare your measured circumference with your calculated circumference.

2. Cut out the calibrated circle to fit inside the rim of your can. Fix it with masking tape rolled sticky-side out.

a. Calculate the length of a table by rolling this can across its surface. Show your work.

b. Now measure the table with your meter tape.

c. Taking the measured value as the accepted table length, find a percent error for your rolling measure.

$\% \text{ error} = \dfrac{\text{difference}}{\text{accepted value}} \times 100$

© 1991 by TOPS Learning Systems   12

Answers / Notes

1-2. Measurements will vary according to can size. Here is one result based on a 15-ounce vegetable can.

1a. d = 7.5 cm. Not knowing the exact center of the can, its difficult to place the diameter of the can with any greater accuracy.

1b. C = πd = 3.14 x 7.5 cm = 23.6 cm.

1c. By actual measurement, C = 23.7 cm. Both values agree in all but the estimated figure, which is uncertain. *(The measured circumference may be slightly higher, since wrapping the meter tape around the can adds to its outer circumference by a small amount.)*

2a. $\dfrac{6.42 \text{ rolls}}{1} \times \dfrac{23.7 \text{ cm}}{1 \text{ roll}} = 152.2 \text{ cm}$

2b. The table equals 152.9 cm by actual measurement.

2c. $\% \text{ error} = \dfrac{0.7 \text{ cm}}{152.9 \text{ cm}} \times 100 = .5\%$

Materials

☐ A can. The hairline can used previously is suitable.
☐ An improvised meter tape.
☐ A circle divided into tenths. Photocopy this from the supplementary page at the pack of this book.
☐ A flat table to measure.
☐ A calculator (optional).

(TO) construct a vernier caliper that accurately measures small distances.

NUTS AND BOLTS (1) ○ Measuring Length ( )

1. Cut out the small 100 unit scale. Fit it to a nut, trimming back the *high end* of the scale until it overlaps just a few units.

2. Glue it evenly around the nut. Overlap so the zero shows.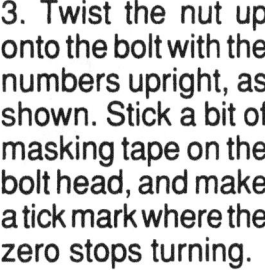

3. Twist the nut up onto the bolt with the numbers upright, as shown. Stick a bit of masking tape on the bolt head, and make a tick mark where the zero stops turning.

4. You have just made a vernier caliper that accurately measures small nonmetric units of distance. Let's call these "vernies."

   a. Firmly close your caliper around each object to measure its thickness in vernies. Complete the table.

Thickness of...	a paper clip	a pin	a penny	a book leaf	aluminum foil
					Measure 10, then divide by 10
# of Vernies					

   b. Measure the *width* of the paper clip. Explain how you did this.

   © 1991 by TOPS Learning Systems

Answers / Notes

4a. *Place each object in the caliper, opposite the tick mark so its thickness can be clearly read.*

Students should not confuse book leaves with book pages (10 leaves = 20 pages).

The easiest way to measure the foil is to cut 5 small pieces and fold them.

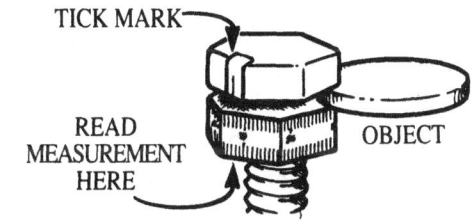

Thickness of...	a paper clip	a pin	a penny	a book leaf	aluminum foil
					Measure 10, then divide by 10
# of Vernies	39	26	62	2.5	.5

4b. The caliper must be turned past zero several times before accommodating the relatively wide paper clip. After firmly fitting the paper clip's width, we found that the caliper turned 50 vernies plus 4 complete revolutions to reclose completely. Since each revolution equals 70 vernies, the paper clip is 50 plus 70 x 4 vernies wide, or 330 vernies.

Materials

☐ A 100 unit caliper scale. Photocopy this from the supplementary page at the back of this book.
☐ Scissors.
☐ A nut and bolt. The calculations above are based on a 5/8 inch size. The caliper scale will adapt to larger or smaller sizes as well. Make sure the nut screws flush against the bolt head. Some don't.
☐ White glue.
☐ Objects to measure: a paper clip, a pin, a penny, leaves in a text book, aluminum foil.

(TO) recalibrate the vernier caliper in metric units and use it to measure short distances.

NUTS AND BOLTS (2) ◯ Measuring Length ( )

1. Accurately cut a 10.0 mm section from your 20 cm ruler.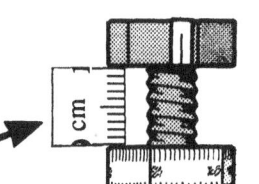

   a. Measure it in vernies with your caliper. Do this several times to estimate your uncertainty.
   b. How many vernies are in 1.0 mm?
   c. How many vernies are in 0.1 mm?

2. Gently peel the vernier scale from its nut. Tape it between notebook paper lines, then draw a new metric scale directly above it.

USE RESULTS FROM 1c.

3. Cut out and glue this new metric scale around the nut.

4. Remeasure each item in significant mm. Is your vernier caliper more accurate than a metric ruler? Explain.

Thickness of...	a paper clip	a pin	a penny	a book leaf	aluminum foil
				Measure 10, then divide by 10	
# of mm					

© 1991 by TOPS Learning Systems

Answers / Notes

1. *These results are based on a 5/8 inch nut and bolt:*
   1a. 10.0 mm = 430 ± 5 vernies *(10 vernies + 6 turns)*
   1b. 1.0 mm = 43 ± .5 vernies
   1c. 0.1 mm = 4.3 ± .05 vernies

2. *Since each tenth millimeter division on the scale spanned a distance of 4.3 vernies, students should draw a metric scale with divisions about this far apart:*

If drawing this small scale is beyond your students' powers of concentration, and if they are using a 5/8 inch bolt similar to ours, the small mm scale on the supplementary page may be substituted in place of calibrating their own.

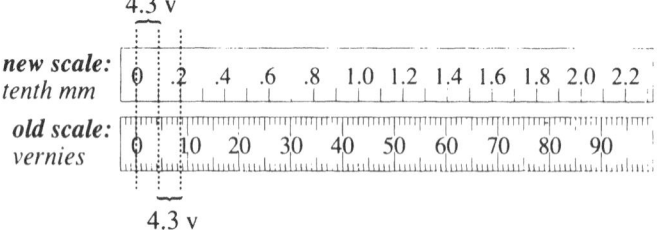

4.

Thickness of...	a paper clip	a pin	a penny	a book leaf	aluminum foil
				Measure 10, then divide by 10	
# of mm	.88	.59	1.40	.057	.012

The vernier caliper is 10 times more accurate. You can estimate between tenth mm lines to an uncertain hundredth. A metric ruler is only estimated between one mm lines to an uncertain tenth.

Materials

☐ The improvised vernier caliper from the previous activity.
☐ The 20 cm ruler. It can be cut up at this point because it has no further use in this module.
☐ The caliper scale divided into tenth mm intervals (optional). Photocopy this from the supplementary page at the back of this book. See note 2, second paragraph, above.
☐ Objects to measure: a paper clip, a pin, a penny, leaves in a text book, aluminum foil.

(TO) learn to convert units of measure by multiplying and dividing so that unwanted units cancel out.

TO THE MOON — Measuring Length ( )

1. Here is a way to find the number of seconds in 1 year.

$$\frac{1 \text{ yr}}{1} \times \frac{365 \text{ da}}{1 \text{ yr}} \times \frac{24 \text{ hr}}{1 \text{ da}} \times \frac{60 \text{ min}}{1 \text{ hr}} \times \frac{60 \text{ sec}}{1 \text{ min}} = 31{,}536{,}000 \text{ sec}$$

Do a similar unit analysis to compute…
   a. the number of mm in 1 km.
   b. the number of inches in 1 mile.

2. Why are metric units easier to compute than English units?

3. Use your vernier caliper to find how many sheets of notebook paper squeeze into 1 mm.

   a. How many sheets of notebook paper reach 1 meter high? Use unit analysis.
   b. The moon is about 400,000 km from Earth. Use a previous answer plus unit analysis to find how many sheet of notebook paper would stack to the moon!

© 1991 by TOPS Learning Systems

Answers / Notes

1. *To convert units, start with what is given: 1 year, in the example; 1 km in part a; 1 mile in part b.*

   1a. $\dfrac{1 \text{ km}}{1} \times \dfrac{1{,}000 \text{ m}}{1 \text{ km}} \times \dfrac{1{,}000 \text{ mm}}{1 \text{ m}} = 1{,}000{,}000 \text{ mm}$

   1b. $\dfrac{1 \text{ mile}}{1} \times \dfrac{5{,}280 \text{ feet}}{1 \text{ mile}} \times \dfrac{12 \text{ inches}}{1 \text{ foot}} = 63{,}360 \text{ inches}$

2. Metric units are easier to convert because they are related by multiples of 10. Multiplying and dividing is simply a matter of moving the decimal point. English units, by contrast, require considerable arithmetic to convert from one unit into another.

3. *These calculations are based on 15 sheets of notebook paper fitting a 1 mm gap:*

   3a. $\dfrac{1 \text{ m}}{1} \times \dfrac{1{,}000 \text{ mm}}{1 \text{ m}} \times \dfrac{15 \text{ sheets}}{1 \text{ mm}} = 15{,}000 \text{ sheets}$

   3b. $400{,}000 \text{ km} \times \dfrac{1{,}000 \text{ m}}{1 \text{ km}} \times \dfrac{15{,}000 \text{ sheets}}{1 \text{ m}} = 6{,}000{,}000{,}000{,}000 \text{ sheets (6 trillion)}$

Discussion

Are you tired of writing big numbers with lots of zeros? Scientific notation provides a short-cut method. Extend this pattern in both directions, 8 lines up and 8 lines down:

$$200 = 2 \times 100 = 2 \times 10^2$$
$$20 = 2 \times 10 = 2 \times 10^1$$
$$2 = 2 \times 1 = 2 \times 10^0$$
$$.2 = 2 \times 1/10 = 2 \times 10^{-1}$$
$$.02 = 2 \times 1/100 = 2 \times 10^{-2}$$

Materials

☐ The improvised vernier caliper from the previous activity calibrated in mm.
☐ Notebook paper. A narrow strip of paper may be accordion-folded into multiple layers.

(TO) project vertical height along the horizontal for easy measurement. To estimate uncertainty in this projection.

LINE OF SIGHT O **Measuring Length (   )**

1. Close one eye. Stand just far enough away from a doorway, with your arm *fully* extended, so your hand span appears exactly as tall as the side of the door frame…

…without moving your body, turn your hand span sideways, projecting the height of the door frame along the base of the wall. Ask your lab partner to mark this distance with masking tape.

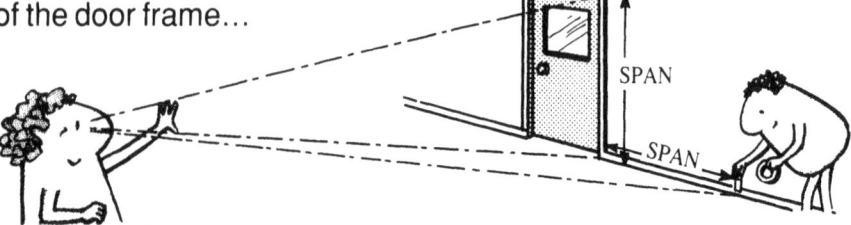

2. Measure both the height of the door frame and its projected distance along the floor in significant figures. Compute your percent error.

$$\% = \frac{\text{difference}}{\text{measured height}} \times 100$$

3. Measure the height of a tall tree (or the corner of a building) using the same projection method.

a. Estimate the uncertainty in your projection based on step 2. Add this to your answer, using plus-or-minus notation.

b. Compare your result with others. Does your estimated uncertainty seem about right?

© 1991 by TOPS Learning Systems

Answers / Notes

Here is one result.

1-2. Height of door frame:
   projected = 207 cm
   measured = 212 cm

   % error = $\frac{5 \text{ cm}}{212 \text{ cm}} \times 100 = 2.4\%$

3. Height of tree:
   3a. projected = 22.6 meters
       estimated error = 22.6 meters x 2.4% = .5 meters
       height plus/minus uncertainty = 22.6 ± .3 meters.

   3b. *Students should list answers from other lab groups and determine whether these values fall within their own estimated uncertainty.*

Materials

☐ A doorway with adjacent clutter-free wall for projecting height. Or substitute a vertical strip of masking tape of comparable height stuck to a bare wall.
☐ Masking tape.
☐ An improvised meter tape.
☐ A tall tree or other outside structure with free space to the side for projecting its height along the horizontal.

REPRODUCIBLE STUDENT TASK CARDS

These Reproducible Student Task Cards may be duplicated for use with this module only, provided such reproductions bear copyright notice. Beyond single-classroom use, reproduction of these task cards by schools or school systems for wider dissemination, or by anyone for commercial sale, is strictly prohibited.

Task Cards Options

Here are 3 management options to consider before you photocopy:

1. Consumable Worksheets: Copy 1 complete set of task card pages. Cut out each card and fix it to a separate sheet of boldly lined paper. Duplicate a class set of each worksheet master you have made, 1 per student. Direct students to follow the task card instructions at the top of each page, then respond to questions in the lined space underneath.

2. Nonconsumable Reference Booklets: Copy and collate the 2-up task card pages in sequence. Make perhaps half as many sets as the students who will use them. Staple each set in the upper left corner, both front and back to prevent the outside pages from working loose. Tell students that these task card booklets are for reference only. They should use them as they would any textbook, responding to questions on their own papers, returning them unmarked and in good shape at the end of the module.

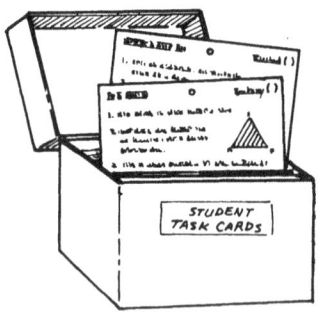

3. Nonconsumable Task Cards: Copy several sets of task card pages. Laminate them, if you wish, for extra durability, then cut out each card to display in your room. You might pin cards to bulletin boards; or punch out the holes and hang them from wall hooks (you can fashion hooks from paper clips and tape these to the wall); or fix cards to cereal boxes with paper fasteners, 4 to a box; or keep cards on designated reference tables. The important thing is to provide enough task card reference points about your classroom to avoid a jam of too many students at any one location. Two or 3 task card sets should accommodate everyone, since different students will use different cards at different times.

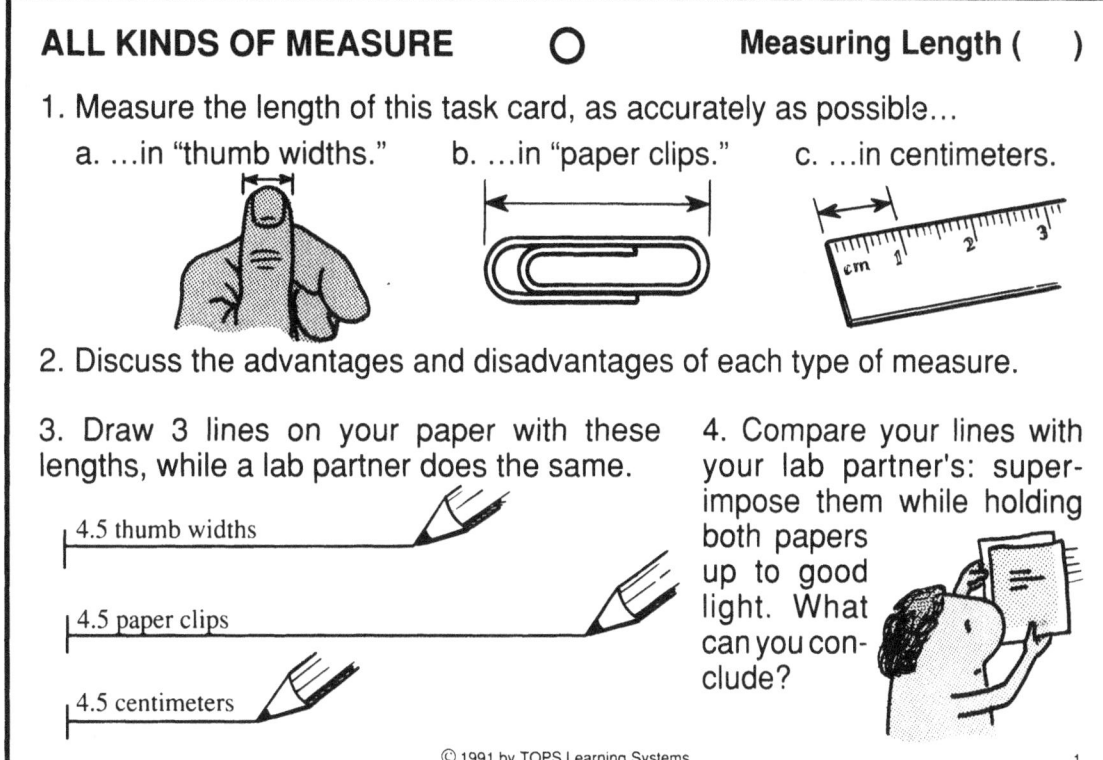

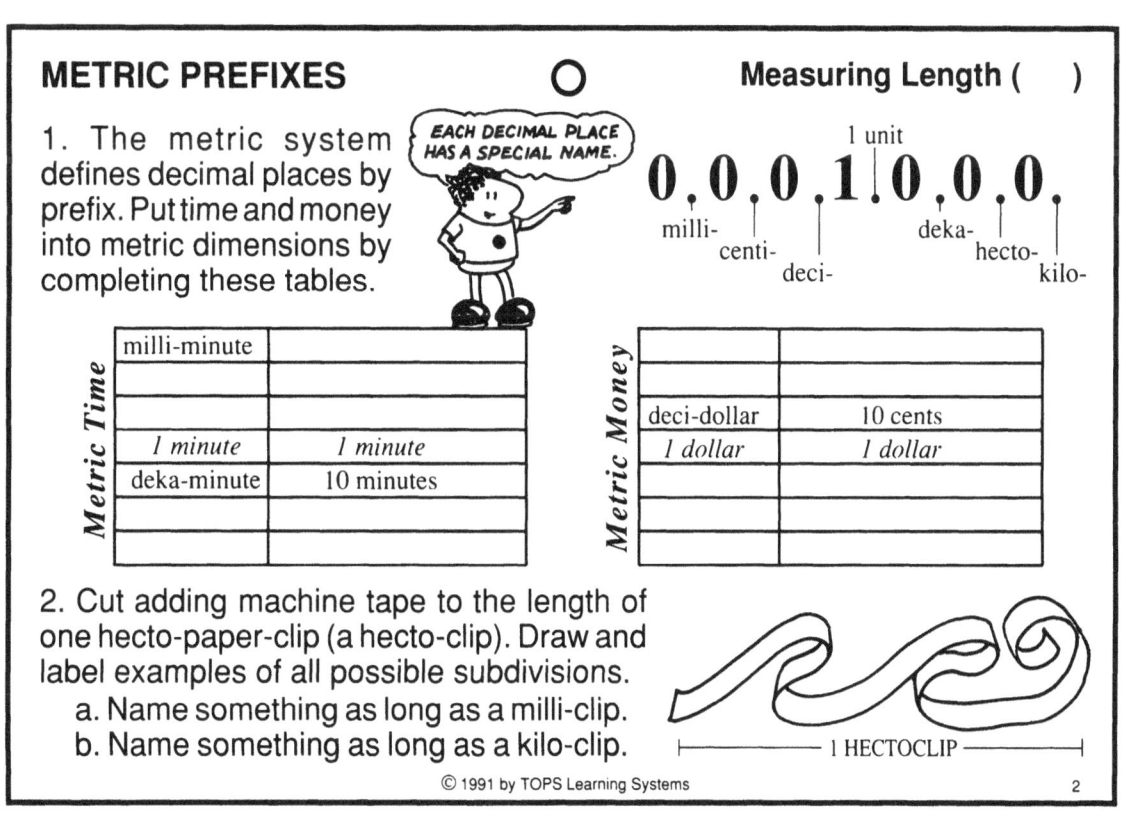

METRIC EQUIVALENTS Measuring Length (   )

1. Carefully cut out a ten-centimeter ruler. No white edge should remain under the small divisions.

2. Use adding machine tape to extend this ruler to one meter. Accurately mark *all* centimeter divisions with the other 20-cm ruler, then number every 5 divisions.

3. Using your ruler as a reference, complete these qualitative and quantitative metric tables. (Label and save your tape for later activities.)

Qualitative			*Quantitative*		
	millimeter				
				1 dm	1/10 meter (.1 m)
	meter	as wide as a doorway		1 m	1 meter (1 m)

4. Complete each equation:

   1 cm = ? mm   1 m = ? cm   1 m = ? mm   1 km = ? m
   1 mm = ? cm   1 cm = ? m   1 mm = ? m   1 m = ? km

© 1991 by TOPS Learning Systems

MILES AND KILOMETERS Measuring Length (   )

1. Cut out a 6 inch ruler (1/2 foot). Use it to cut exactly one *milli*-mile of string. Explain how you did this.

2. Your milli-mile string is what fraction of a mile? Your meter tape is what fraction of a kilometer?

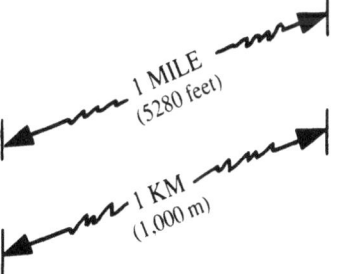

3. Your milli-mile string and meter tape are equally scaled-down versions of a full mile and a full kilometer.
   a. Which is longer, a kilometer or a mile?
   b. How many times does the shorter fit into the longer? (Round off to 2 digits.)

4. Complete this conversion table.

5. A highway speed limit is 60 mph. Convert this to kph.

MILE	KILOMETER
1	
10	
	8
	160

© 1991 by TOPS Learning Systems

ESTIMATE THE LAST DIGIT ○ Measuring Length ( )

1. Write the correct measure for each letter. Always make the last digit zero when the hairline hits the mark dead center.

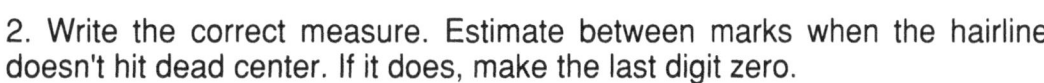
g   d   f   h   b   c   e   j   i   a = 12.20 cm

2. Write the correct measure. Estimate between marks when the hairline doesn't hit dead center. If it does, make the last digit zero.

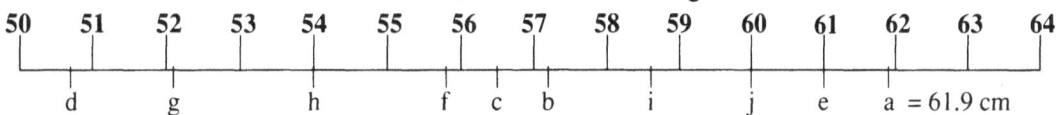
d   g   h   f   c   b   i   j   e   a = 61.9 cm

3. Write the correct measure. Apply the rules you learned above when writing the last digit.

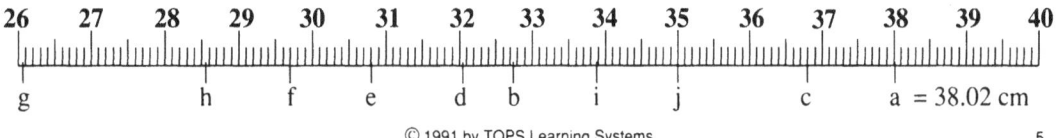
g   h   f   e   d   b   i   j   c   a = 38.02 cm

SIGNIFICANT FIGURES ○ Measuring Length ( )

1. The last digit in any good measurement is estimated, and therefore uncertain. Write *two* possible measurements for each letter.

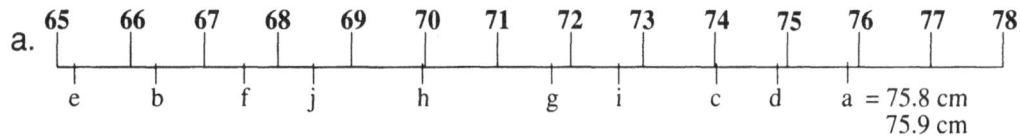
a. e   b   f   j   h   g   i   c   d   a = 75.8 cm
                                           75.9 cm

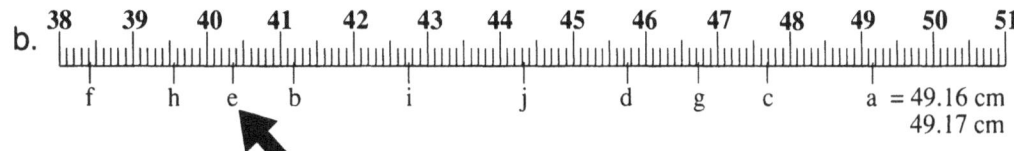
b. f   h   e   b   i   j   d   g   c   a = 49.16 cm
                                           49.17 cm

2. Five students gave these measurements for letter "e" above: 40.36 cm, 43.60 cm, 40.37 cm, 40.36 cm, 40.35 cm. Are all these measurements valid? Explain.

3. Any valid measurement contains only significant figures. What are significant figures?

4. Is it possible to calibrate a ruler so accurately that measuring uncertainty is eliminated? Explain.

HAIRLINE MEASURE   Measuring Length (   )

1. Cut out the ruled rectangle on the dashed line. Wrap it around a can, taping the ends to the metal surface with 1 long piece of tape.

2. Cut out a 4 cm x 26 cm band of waxed paper and wrap it very *snugly* over the rectangle. Tape it to itself so the band remains free to slide.

3. Tape a dark strand of straight hair across the waxed band. Line it up with the vertical line at the beginning of the rulers.

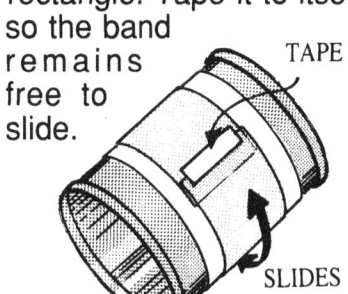
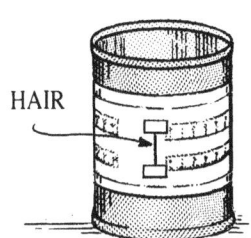

4. Move your hairline along the *lower* mm divisions, stopping at these intervals. Describe your trip.
   a. 12.00, 12.10, 12.20, 12.30, 12.40, 12.50, 12.60, ..., 13.00.
   b. 12.00, 12.01, 12.02, 12.03, 12.04, 12.05, 12.06, ..., 12.10.

5. Repeat your journey of 4a and 4b along the *upper* cm divisions.

© 1991 by TOPS Learning Systems   7

AGREE / DISAGREE (1)   Measuring Length (   )

1. Work with a lab partner. Fold a clean sheet of notebook paper in half. Number along the fold, and paper clip as shown.

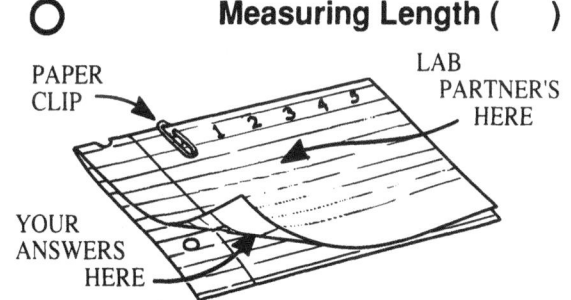

2. Play agree / disagree on the *upper* cm divisions of your can.

   a. DIAL any random measure without looking at the hairline.
   b. WRITE the hairline measurement in significant figures. You use the *inside* of the paper, while your lab partner writes an independent answer on the *outside*.
   c. COMPARE answers inside and out. Advance the paper clip by 1 number if you agree (estimated digit off by no more than one). Slide back 2 numbers if you disagree (estimated digit off by more than one, or certain digits disagree). Play until you reach 5.

3. Repeat this game on the *lower* mm divisions of your can.

4. Which scale is hardest to play? Why?

© 1991 by TOPS Learning Systems   8

AGREE / DISAGREE (2) Measuring Length ( )

1. Fold, number and paper clip a clean sheet of notebook paper from 0 to 5 as before. Use a 20 cm paper ruler to play another game of agree / disagree: MEASURE each line independently; COMPARE answers; SLIDE the paper clip forward or back, following previous rules.

```
a. ─────────────────────────────────
         b. ──────────────────────────
   c. ─────────────────────
      e. ──────────  d. ──────────
          f. ─────────────────
             g. ────────────
          h. ──────────────────────
i. ────────────────────────────────────
   j. ──────────
   l. ──── k. ──────────────────
       m. ───────────────────────────
```

  a. Is the game easier to play with a ruler or with a hairline? Explain.
  b. How would you revise the game rules to make it easier to win?

2. Uncertainty in a measurement can be expressed as "plus or minus." The length of line m (the bottom line) expressed in this way is 9.91 ± .01 cm.
  a. List 3 possible line lengths given by this number.
  b. Does 9.92 ± .01 cm agree with 9.90 ± .01 cm? Explain.
  c. Try another game, writing measurements with an uncertainty (± .01).

© 1991 by TOPS Learning Systems

NORM AVERAGE Measuring Length ( )

1. Work with a lab partner to measure each length 3 times in significant figures. (Don't let the results of one trial influence your measurement in the next.) Use these trials to estimate the uncertainty in each measurement.

	trial 1	trail 2	trial 3	average ± uncertainty
fathom				
height				
forearm				
foot				
span				

2. These equations fit the body proportions of Norm Average. How well do they fit you? (Note: In part c, multiplying a measurement also multiplies its uncertainty.)
  a. fathom = height   b. forearm = foot   c. 8 spans = fathom

© 1991 by TOPS Learning Systems

LONG AND SHORT ○ **Measuring Length ( )**

1. Find each measure below. Be sure to:
   ...use the best unit (mm, cm, m or km).
   ...express each measure in significant figures.
   ...estimate uncertainty using plus-or-minus notation.

   a. Width of a sheet of notebook paper.
   b. Distance from your school to the state capitol building.
   c. Length of your classroom.
   d. Thickness of a penny.

   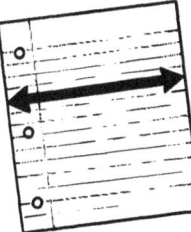
   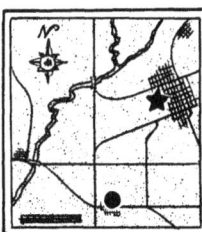

2. Justify your uncertainty for each measure above. Explain why you chose the numbers you did.

3. Can you think of ways to reduce the uncertainty in any of these measures? Explain.

© 1991 by TOPS Learning Systems

ROLLING MEASURE ○ **Measuring Length ( )**

1. Get an empty can. Call its diameter "d" and its circumference "C."

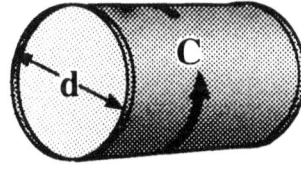

a. Measure d with your meter tape to an accuracy of 0.1 cm. Why can't you be more accurate than this?

b. Calculate C using this formula:
$$C = \pi d = 3.14\, d$$

c. Now measure C with your meter tape. Compare your measured circumference with your calculated circumference.

2. Cut out the calibrated circle to fit inside the rim of your can. Fix it with masking tape rolled sticky-side out.

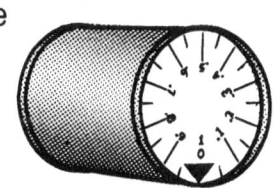

a. Calculate the length of a table by rolling this can across its surface. Show your work.

b. Now measure the table with your meter tape.

c. Taking the measured value as the accepted table length, find a percent error for your rolling measure.

$$\%\ \text{error} = \frac{\text{difference}}{\text{accepted value}} \times 100$$

© 1991 by TOPS Learning Systems

NUTS AND BOLTS (1)   Measuring Length (   )

1. Cut out the small 100 unit scale. Fit it to a nut, trimming back the *high end* of the scale until it overlaps just a few units.

2. Glue it evenly around the nut. Overlap so the zero shows.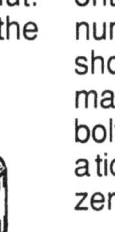

3. Twist the nut up onto the bolt with the numbers upright, as shown. Stick a bit of masking tape on the bolt head, and make a tick mark where the zero stops turning.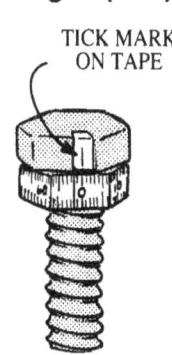

TICK MARK ON TAPE

4. You have just made a vernier caliper that accurately measures small nonmetric units of distance. Let's call these "vernies."

   a. Firmly close your caliper around each object to measure its thickness in vernies. Complete the table.

Thickness of...	a paper clip	a pin	a penny	a book leaf	aluminum foil
				Measure 10, then divide by 10	
# of Vernies					

   b. Measure the *width* of the paper clip. Explain how you did this.

NUTS AND BOLTS (2)   Measuring Length (   )

1. Accurately cut a 10.0 mm section from your 20 cm ruler.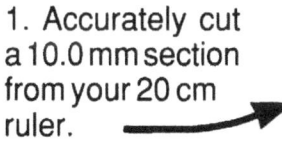

2. Gently peel the vernier scale from its nut. Tape it between notebook paper lines, then draw a new metric scale directly above it.

   a. Measure it in vernies with your caliper. Do this several times to estimate your uncertainty.
   b. How many vernies are in 1.0 mm?
   c. How many vernies are in 0.1 mm?

USE RESULTS FROM 1c.

3. Cut out and glue this new metric scale around the nut.

4. Remeasure each item in significant mm. Is your vernier caliper more accurate than a metric ruler? Explain.

Thickness of...	a paper clip	a pin	a penny	a book leaf	aluminum foil
				Measure 10, then divide by 10	
# of mm					

TO THE MOON   O   Measuring Length (   )

1. Here is a way to find the number of seconds in 1 year.

$$\frac{1 \cancel{yr}}{1} \times \frac{365 \cancel{da}}{1 \cancel{yr}} \times \frac{24 \cancel{hr}}{1 \cancel{da}} \times \frac{60 \cancel{min}}{1 \cancel{hr}} \times \frac{60 \text{ sec}}{1 \cancel{min}} = 31{,}536{,}000 \text{ sec}$$

Do a similar unit analysis to compute...
   a. the number of mm in 1 km.
   b. the number of inches in 1 mile.

2. Why are metric units easier to compute than English units?

3. Use your vernier caliper to find how many sheets of notebook paper squeeze into 1 mm.

   a. How many sheets of notebook paper reach 1 meter high? Use unit analysis.
   b. The moon is about 400,000 km from Earth. Use a previous answer plus unit analysis to find how many sheet of notebook paper would stack to the moon!

LINE OF SIGHT   O   Measuring Length (   )

1. Close one eye. Stand just far enough away from a doorway, with your arm *fully* extended, so your hand span appears exactly as tall as the side of the door frame... ...without moving your body, turn your hand span sideways, projecting the height of the door frame along the base of the wall. Ask your lab partner to mark this distance with masking tape.

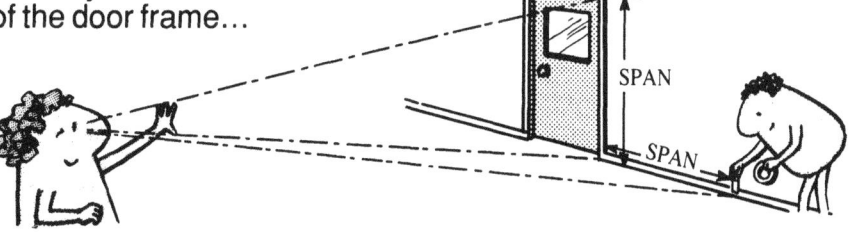

2. Measure both the height of the door frame and its projected distance along the floor in significant figures. Compute your percent error.

$$\% = \frac{\text{difference}}{\text{measured height}} \times 100$$

3. Measure the height of a tall tree (or the corner of a building) using the same projection method.

   a. Estimate the uncertainty in your projection based on step 2. Add this to your answer, using plus-or-minus notation.
   b. Compare your result with others. Does your estimated uncertainty seem about right?

SUPPLEMENTARY PAGES

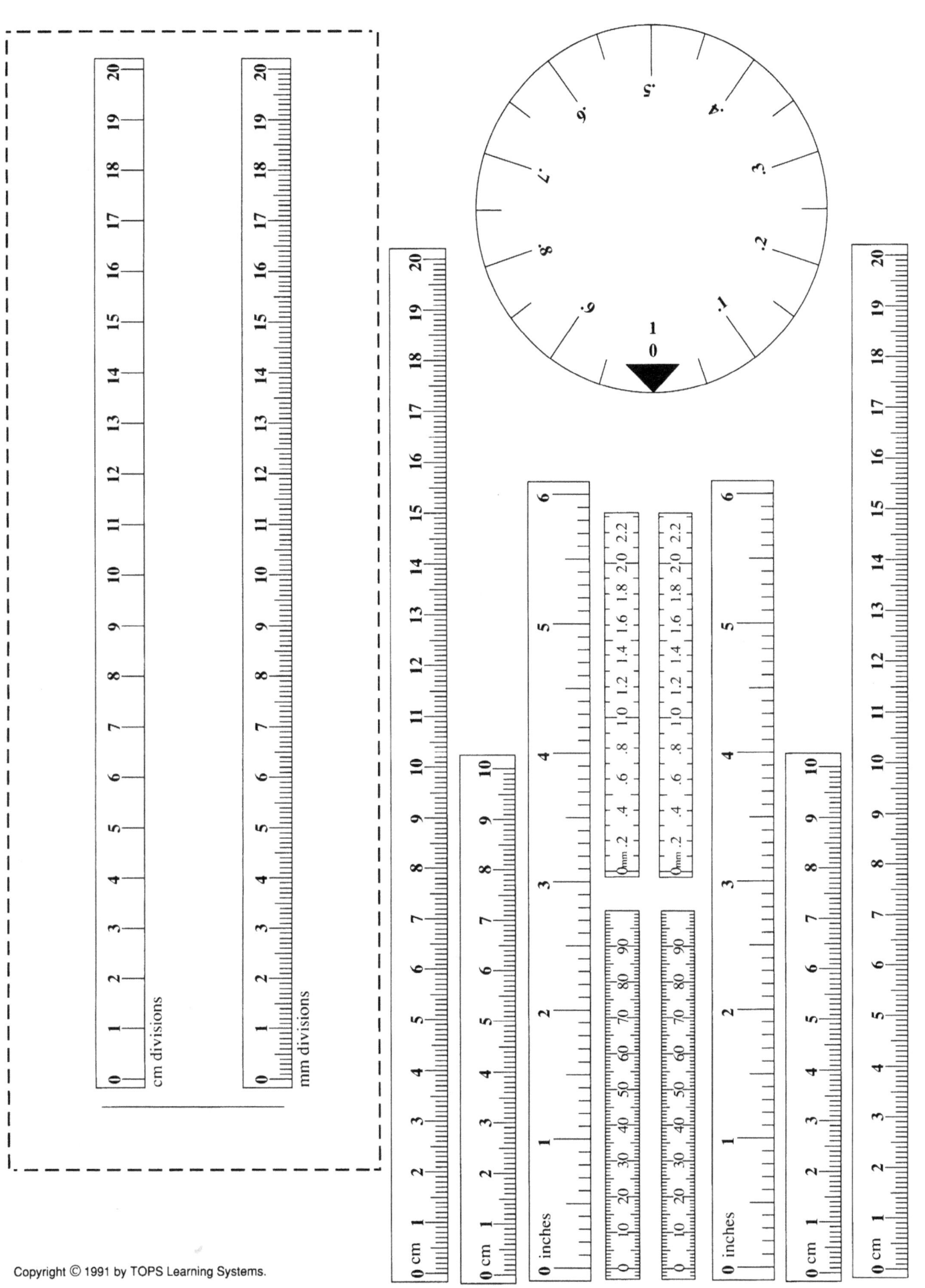

Feedback

If you enjoyed teaching TOPS please tell us so. Your praise motivates us to work hard. If you found an error or can suggest ways to improve this module, we need to hear about that too. Your criticism will help us improve our next new edition. Would you like information about our other publications? Ask us to send you our latest catalog free of charge.

For whatever reason, we'd love to hear from you. We include this self-mailer for your convenience.

Sincerely,

Ron & Peg

Ron and Peg Marson
author and illustrator

Your Message Here:

Module Title _____ Date _____

Name _____ School _____

Address _____

City _____ State _____ Zip _____

———————————————— FIRST FOLD ————————————————

———————————————— SECOND FOLD ————————————————

RETURN ADDRESS

_____

_____

_____

PLACE
STAMP
HERE

TOPS Learning Systems
342 S Plumas St
Willows, CA 95988

TAPE HERE

www.ingramcontent.com/pod-product-compliance
Lightning Source LLC
Chambersburg PA
CBHW081926170426
43200CB00014B/2846